MOTHER TONGUES AND
OTHER REFLECTIONS ON THE ITALIAN LANGUAGE

TORONTO ITALIAN STUDIES

Goggio Publication Series
General Editor: Olga Zorzi Pugliese

GIULIO LEPSCHY

# Mother Tongues
and Other Reflections
on the Italian Language

UNIVERSITY OF TORONTO PRESS
Toronto Buffalo London

© University of Toronto Press Incorporated 2002
Toronto  Buffalo  London
Printed in Canada

ISBN 0-8020-3729-1

Printed on acid-free paper

**National Library of Canada Cataloguing in Publication**

Lepschy, Giulio C.
Mother tongues and other reflections on the Italian language/Giulio Lepschy.

(Toronto Italian studies)
(Goggio publications series)
Includes bibliographical references and index
ISBN 0-8020-3729-1

1. Italian philology.   2. Veniexiana.   3. Dionisotti, Carlo.   I. Title.
II. Series.   III. Series: Goggio publications series.

PC1711.L46 2002      450      C2002-903422-1

This book has been published with the help of a grant from the Emilio Goggio
Chair in Italian Studies, Department of Italian Studies, University of Toronto.

University of Toronto Press acknowledges the financial assistance to its
publishing program of the Canada Council for the Arts and the Ontario
Arts Council.

University of Toronto Press acknowledges the financial support for its publishing
activities of the Government of Canada through the Book Publishing Industry
Development Program (BPIDP).

# Contents

# Foreword

The Department of Italian Studies at the University of Toronto had the pleasure of hosting Professor Giulio Lepschy as the Emilio Goggio Visiting Professor in Italian Studies for the year 2000. Originally from Venice and now professor emeritus of the University of Reading and honorary professor at University College London, Giulio Lepschy is the author of many studies on Italian linguistics and also on the history of linguistics (e.g., *A History of Linguistics* in four volumes). He spent one academic term in the department together with his wife, Laura, also a recently retired professor of Italian from University College London. During their stay in Toronto both Giulio and Laura Lepschy agreed to be interviewed by the local Italian-language press. Articles on them, including photos, appeared in the 21 October 2000 issue of the Toronto-based *Corriere Canadese* (and an English version in that paper's weekly publication, *Tandem*, the next day).

As Emilio Goggio Visiting Professor in the Department, Giulio Lepschy taught a graduate course on 'Aspects of the Italian Language' and also delivered three public lectures on 5, 13, and 19 October 2000. The specific titles of his talks, which were accessible, learned, and witty, were as follows: 'Popular Italian: Fact or Fiction?'; 'The Languages of Italy'; '*La Veniexiana*: A Venetian Play of the Renaissance,' the latter co-sponsored with the Centre for Reformation and Renaissance Studies (Victoria College). The texts of Professor Lepschy's lectures are published here together with three other pieces on the concept of mother tongues, secondary stress in Italian, and a memoir on the late scholar Carlo Dionisotti.

The Emilio Goggio Publication Series, in which these studies now appear, has been made possible through the continued support of the members of the Goggio family, especially Mr Ernest Goggio. They established the Goggio chair in the department of Italian Studies in 1995 in honour of their mother Emma and their father Emilio Goggio, who had been chair of the department of Italian and Spanish at the University of Toronto from 1946 to 1956. The endowment of the Goggio Chair was intended to support activities that promote research in Italian studies. As the third contribution by a distinguished Italianist to the Goggio Publication Series, Giulio Lepschy's *Mother Tongues and Other Reflections on the Italian Language* reflects those basic aims, providing valuable insights into the very core of Italian culture, namely, its language.

Grateful acknowledgment is made to Grace Wright for her assistance in the preparation of the typescript of this volume.

Olga Zorzi Pugliese
Chair, Department of Italian Studies, and
Emilio Goggio Chair in Italian Studies

# *Preface*

This book presents, as chapters two, three and five, the Goggio Public Lectures I gave at the University of Toronto in the autumn of 2000. I have added three other chapters on topics related to my public lectures or discussed with my graduate students in Toronto. In spite of the apparent disparity of the six topics, I think they offer a coherent illustration of some of my main interests.[1]

In chapter one I examine the notions of 'mother tongue' and 'native speaker,' underlining their centrality for modern linguistic theory, tracing some episodes in their complex earlier history, and identifying the particularly problematic aspect they acquire in an Italian context; finally, I touch on their intriguing links with the notions of poetic and literary language.

In chapters two and three I bring together much of the work I have done on the linguistic situation of modern Italy: the variety of idioms used, from regional dialects to 'foreign' tongues, and the spread of that ordinary, more demotic language, which has been dubbed 'popular Italian.'

In chapter four I put forward some of the hypotheses on an aspect of modern Italian phonology, that of secondary stress, which I developed as I was collaborating with Tullio De Mauro in the preparation of the large *Dizionario italiano dell'uso* published by UTET (Unione Tipografico-Editrice Torinese) in 1999.

The last two chapters exemplify different aspects of my interests, including dialectology and the history of linguistic and philological thought. In chaper five I discuss an extraordinary sixteenth-century text, *La Veniexiana*, which is one of the most powerful and original plays of the Renaissance. Here, I examine in detail a new interpretation of a passage, which throws light on questions of 'gender' in the play. This interpretation is based on a reading proposed by one of the greatest historians of Italian literature, Carlo Dionisotti. In chapter six I present a profile of Dionisotti's life and work.

I should like to express my gratitude to Professor Olga Zorzi Pugliese, who invited me to be Emilio Goggio Visiting Professor. I found my stay in Toronto enormously enjoyable, fruitful, and stimulating, thanks to the cordiality of both colleagues and graduate students of the Department of Italian Studies in Toronto, and the extraordinary quality of the libraries there, both the Robarts and that of the Pontifical Institute of Mediaeval Studies (PIMS). I should also like to add that most of the work on which these studies are based was done in collaboration with my wife, Anna Laura (who also taught in Toronto during our stay). The extent of our cooperation is clear from the many publications that we have signed together.

Giulio Lepschy
Toronto, London, Venice, 2000–1

NOTE

1 Chapter one is the text of the Presidential Address to the Modern Humanities Research Association, delivered on 16 March 2001, which will be published in *Modern Language Review* 96, pt 4. Chapter four will appear in a Danish Festschrift: *L'infinito & oltre. Omaggio a Gunver Skytte* (Odense: Odense University Press, 2002). Chapter six is reproduced by permission from *Proceedings of the British Academy*, vol. 11 (2000), © The British Academy 2001. Chapters two, three, and five are based on the three public lectures delivered in Toronto on 13, 5, and 19 October 2000, respectively. I am grateful to Paolo Rambelli and Helena Sanson for their help in the preparation of this volume.

MOTHER TONGUES AND
OTHER REFLECTIONS ON THE ITALIAN LANGUAGE

# CHAPTER ONE

# Mother Tongues and Literary Languages

Native speaker and mother tongue are two symmetrical and converse notions. They seem to refer to the same reality from two opposite viewpoints. Native speakers, by definition, speak their mother tongue, and a mother tongue is the language of a native speaker. In spite of this correspondence, the implications and the history of these two designations are very different; for both expressions part of the difficulty lies in the relation they have to the notion of literary language.

In this chapter I shall discuss four points: (1) native speaker, (2) mother tongue, (3) the births and deaths of languages, and (4) literary language, and in what sense the four are connected. I shall look, in particular, at topics emerging in the context of Latin, Hebrew, and Italian. This chapter is written from the perspective of someone who is predominantly a linguist but is also interested in the literary aspect of the questions under discussion. It is my belief that, although the two approaches, the linguistic and the literary, are distinct, they can only gain from being linked, and in some cases they inevitably suffer from being kept apart.

## 1. *Native Speaker*

The notion of native speaker seems to be central for modern linguistics. This centrality is usually traced back to Leonard Bloomfield, who in his 1933 monograph titled *Language* noted that 'The first language a human being learns to speak is his *native language*;

he is a *native speaker* of that language,'[1] and to Noam Chomsky, who in his *Syntactic Structures*, published in 1957, stated that grammatical sentences have to be 'acceptable to a native speaker.'[2] With the two most influential American linguists of the twentieth century (one considered the main representative of structural linguistics, the other the founder of generative linguistics) using the native speaker as a basis on which the whole of linguistic theory rests, one might be justified in expecting the notion to have been clearly defined and analysed in great detail and its previous history to have been satisfactorily traced.

This is far from being the case. Several volumes have been devoted to the native speaker during the last two decades,[3] but the notion remains elusive and hazy and its history difficult to ascertain. The *Oxford English Dictionary* (OED) does not record it either under 'native' or under 'speaker'; the CD-ROM of the second edition (1989) provides seventeen hits under different entries, dated between 1942 and 1982 and irrelevant for our purposes. Together with Helena Sanson, a colleague in the Italian department at University College London, I have done some work on the history of the expressions 'native speaker' and 'mother tongue.'[4] We were struck by a concentration of examples of 'native speaker' in the first years of the twentieth century in the debates concerning the revival of Irish. The expressions 'Irish speaker' and 'native (Irish) speaker' seem to be more or less interchangeable, in the context of these discussions.[5]

If the OED is not very helpful for tracing the history of the phrase 'native speaker,'[6] bilingual dictionaries are obviously useless for this purpose, apart from confirming the peculiarity of the English designation by either offering translations which are clearly calqued on English (such as the French *locuteur natif*, the Spanish *hablante nativo*, the Italian *parlante nativo*), or having recourse to different expressions involving the mother tongue (see the German

*Muttersprachler(in)* or the Italian *il/la madrelingua* for persons who speak or teach their mother tongue). This subject needs to be examined more closely.

## 2. *Mother Tongue*

### 2.1. *English*
The expressions *mother tongue* and *mother language* are recorded in the OED with two separate senses. The first is 'one's native language.' Both for *mother tongue* and for *mother language* the earliest attestation is found in Wyclif (1380). With the second sense ('an original language from which others spring') the earliest quotation for *mother tongue* occurs in 1645 and for *mother language* in 1680. Some interesting transferred usages are also quoted, in which *mother tongue* seems to acquire more universal resonances, for instance, in Gibbon (III, 15 n., 1781), for whom Shakespeare's mother tongue, 'the language of nature, is the same in Cappadocia and in Britain'; and in 1865 we find that 'The mother-tongue of the deaf and dumb, is the language of signs.'

For the expression *mother tongue* in sense 1 (native language), according to the OED: '*mother* was originally the uninflected genitive,' and attestations with *mothers* are indicated (1540, 1617). In the entry for *mother* there are also other combinations 'imitated' from *mother tongue,* such as *mother speache* (1603) and *mother dialect* (1644).

### 2.2. *German*
The German expression *Muttersprache* has a more fraught history. A recent volume by C.M. Hutton[7] offers a disturbing and depressing analysis of the nazification of German linguistics and comparative philology in the 1930s and, even more worrying, of how effortless this process was, owing to the close association, particu-

larly during the nineteenth century, between the notion of mother tongue and German nationalism. Fortified with the Humboldtian idea that different languages were naturally linked to different world views, it is not surprising that the exaltation of the mother tongue should have led to Leo Weisgerber's *Muttersprache und Geistesbildung*[8] and, even worse, to Georg Schmidt-Rohr's *Mutter Sprache*.[9] The origin of the expression *Mutter Sprache* is controversial. The traditional view[10] is that it is a calque on the Medieval Latin *lingua materna*, but Leo Weisgerber[11] has argued that it is a German rather than a Romance coinage. The attestation quoted of *materna lingua*, at the beginning of the twelfth century (1119, to be precise),[12] is by Hesso 'magister scholarum argentinensis,' that is, a school master from Argentorate, or Strasburg, who, according to Weisgerber, must have based the Latin phrase on a native German expression, *Mutter Sprache*. Leo Spitzer[13] objected, first, on grounds of historical documentation: the Latin attestations from the twelfth century are earlier than the German ones from the fourteenth century.[14] His second objection was one of cultural history: the Latin expression is related to the importance attributed in the Latin Middle Ages to maternal education. Third, he objected on grounds of grammatical analysis: *Mutter* in *Mutter Sprache*, is more likely to be a genitive ('the language of the mother') than a prefix (as in for example *Mutterboden*, *Muttererde*, *Mutterland*, etc.) meaning 'acting like a mother.'

It has been pointed out that Weisgerber projects onto the Middle Ages certain connotations that emerged only later.[15] In fact, Heymann Steinthal in an 1867 article comments on the late development of this notion in Germany and observes that the 'love for the mother tongue' requires both culture (the uneducated seem to lack the concept) and the presence of the 'other,' that is, a contrast between the mother tongue and a different language.[16] The Greeks, who produced the most developed culture in antiquity, had notoriously little interest in foreign languages, and, according to Steinthal, not only did they not show any 'love' for their own mother tongue, but they did not even know the phrase 'mother tongue.'

## 2.3. *Italian*

In Italian the terms *nativo* and *natio* are frequently found in collocations with words belonging to the sphere of linguistic expressions. For instance, in Dante's *Inferno* (10, 25–7) Farinata tells the poet: 'Your speech makes it clear that you are a native of that noble land to which I was perhaps too hostile' (La tua loquela ti fa manifesto / di quella nobil patria natio / a la qual forse fui troppo molesto).

Benedetto Varchi notes: 'Native languages, which we call our own, are those which are spoken naturally, that is are learnt without studying them and almost without realizing it, through hearing nurses, mothers, fathers, and the other inhabitants of the neighbourhood speak, those in sum which can be said to be sucked with the mother's milk and acquired in the cradle' (Lingue natie, le quali noi chiamiamo proprie e nostrali, sono quelle le quali naturalmente si favellano, cioè s'imparano senza porvi alcuno studio e quasi non se ne accorgendo, nel sentire favellare le balie, le madri, i padri, e l'altre genti della contrada, e quelle, in somma le quali si suol dire che si succiano col latte e s'apprendono nella culla).[17]

The Italian equivalent of *mother tongue* has two different forms: (a) *madre lingua* and (b) *lingua madre*. Both can be written as one word (this is more common for *madrelingua*), or two words (this is more common for *lingua madre*). Both expressions can mean (as we saw for *mother tongue*) either (1) 'native language' (this sense is more common for *madre lingua*), or (2) 'language from which others spring' (this sense is more common for *lingua madre*). For both expressions the second sense, 'language from which others spring,' is attested earlier than the first, 'native language,' which seems to be documented only from the nineteenth century.

As for the second sense ('language from which others spring'), it is less relevant for my purpose here, and I shall observe only that Battaglia, s.v. *lingua madre*, gives quotes from 1549 (Giambullari) to 1785 (Cesarotti) that seem to include the word *madre* in the relevant sense, but not the collocation *lingua madre*. The earliest attestation is from Lanzi (1789), who gives both *lingua madre* and *madre lingua*. In the latest edition of Cortelazzo and Zolli, *Dizionario*, an earlier attestation, from Magalotti (1711), is quoted.[18]

## 3. Births and Deaths of Languages

### 3.1. Beginnings and Ends

One problem that cannot be avoided in this context (as well as, it must be said, in most questions involving language) is that of the dichotomy between synchrony and diachrony. Do languages have a beginning and an end? We live in times in which beginnings and ends seem to appear where they are least expected, or rather (which is perhaps not quite the same), things suddenly acquire birth or death certificates.

In reference works one finds that for famous people of the past the date of birth is more frequently unknown than the date of death. For humans, as well as for historical phenomena, it is usually more difficult to establish the beginning – for the obvious reason that one does not know from the start whether something is worth recording. Philip Larkin, however, had the good fortune to discover that 'Sexual intercourse began / In nineteen sixty-three / (Which was rather late for me) – / Between the end of the *Chatterley* ban / and the Beatles' first LP.'[19] As for the endings, we all have had to record many sad losses. God died, and Nietzsche wrote the obituary in 1882: 'Gott ist todt.'[20] The author died too, Roland Barthes announcing *La mort de l'auteur* in 1968.[21]

Regarding the extinction of languages, when I was a student, half a century ago, it seemed to be a rare occurrence. In Italy all students of Romance linguistics learnt that the last native speaker of Dalmatic, Antonio Udina Burbur, had died in 1898, 'after the dialect was recorded and preserved for science' (dopo che il dialetto aveva potuto essere raccolto e salvato alla scienza) in the two volumes by Matteo Bartoli, published in Vienna in 1906.[22]

Today we are far more aware of this phenomenon, and we consider it with less equanimity, concerned as we are about the preservation of the biosphere. In the year 2000 two books were published on the topic of the extinction of languages. Both are good, informative, and highly depressing, one by Daniel Nettle and Suzanne Romaine[23] and the other by David Crystal.[24] From both we can glean a long list of 'last native speakers' around the world, which marks a sad roll-call for dying languages.

Dead languages may even become extinct again, metaphorically speaking. In 1998 the great Romance linguist Yakov Malkiel died; he had often described himself as the last surviving native speaker of Old Portuguese. This paradoxical designation was, of course, jocular, but it pointed to the intimate knowledge that one may have of a dead language. It may also suggest that, in appropriate circumstances, a language might be renativized and native speakers be born again, as we shall see.

In general, the birth of languages is even less well understood than the death of languages. In 1960 an interesting exhibition took place in Florence to celebrate the thousandth year of the Italian language. The reference was, of course, to the first dated document in an Italian vernacular, the *Placito Capuano* of 960, that is, the account, in Latin, of a court case in which witnesses state that they know that certain lands belong to the convent of St Benedict: 'Sao ko kelle terre,' and so on. This is the earliest dated document, but obviously it does not tell us when Italian (or rather the vernacular) started being spoken.

### 3.2. *Latin and Vernacular*

There is a long-drawn-out discussion, almost a cause célèbre, concerning the question, 'à quelle époque a-t-on cessé de parler latin?'[25] This question, of course, is not about language death, partly because Latin survived for centuries as a written language (and is still used in certain circumstances), and partly because, as a spoken language, it was transformed into the Romance vernaculars. From another viewpoint, it seems clear that there was a period of overlap, in which Latin and Romance coexisted, and therefore 'When did spoken Latin die?' and 'When was the vernacular born?' are distinct questions, which may receive different answers.

They are also asymmetric questions in another way. We have seen that it is common to associate the death of a language with the death of its last native speakers. Yet it is more difficult to associate the birth of a language with the birth of its first native speakers, since children's innate linguistic ability must be activated by some language that is already in use at the time of their birth.

### 3.3. *Latin Reborn*

The examples from Latin illustrate the case of idioms that are used as written rather than spoken languages in a diglossic society. One assumes that from the period in late antiquity in which people ceased speaking Latin, even though they kept it as a written, literary language, there were no longer any Latin native speakers. This, in some sense, must be true, notwithstanding some examples that are quoted to the contrary, for instance, in Ferdinand Brunot's history of the French language, an influential source that is often invoked in this context.[26]

The best-known instance of a native speaker of Latin in the Renaissance is that of Montaigne, who in his *Essais* (Book I, chap. 26) relates how his father thought that the knowledge of classical languages was indeed indispensable, but an excessive amount of time was required to learn it through a traditional curriculum of study. He therefore decided to make his son learn Latin as his first language. In 1535 Michel, who was just over two years old, was entrusted to a German pedagogue who could not speak French and had been instructed (together with two other helpers) to use only Latin with the infant. All the other members of the family, including the mother and the servants, were also ordered to use exclusively the Latin words they had learnt for this purpose. 'As for me,' says Montaigne, 'I was over six years old before I heard a word of French or Perigordin any more than Arabic' (Quant à moy, j'avois plus de six ans avant que j'entendisse non plus de François ou de Perigordin que d'Arabesque).[27] This was to no avail, however, since no sooner was he sent to the Collège de Guienne at the age of six than his Latin became irreparably bastardized and was later abandoned for lack of practice.

According to Roger Trinquet,[28] this unsuccessful attempt to make Montaigne a native speaker of Latin was stimulated by the prestige of Erasmus's work, *Declamatio de pueris statim ac liberaliter instituendis* (1529). Erasmus suggests that children will always learn the vernacular: 'There is no danger that they do not acquire the vernacular, they will learn it willy nilly through dealings with ordinary people' (Nec est periculum ne populi linguam ignorent, eam perdiscent velint nolint hominum commercio). The sooner Latin is taught, through the use of Latin, the better: 'Besides, the earlier children are entrusted to an educator, the more successful their formation will be' (Porro quo maturius puer tradetur formatori, hoc felicius succedet institutio).[31] 'First of all, the use of language ... happens without any effort in children, whereas in adults this faculty is acquired, if at all, with great effort' (Primum linguarum usus ... qui citra studium omne contingit infantibus, quum adultis ea facultas vix ingenti studio comparetur).[29]

In 1535, the same year in which the two-year-old Montaigne began his Latin education, Clenardus (the Flemish philologist Nicolaus van der Beke, author of a famous Greek grammar, as well as of Latin and Hebrew manuals) wrote from Evora in Portugal a letter to Rutger Rescius (another Flemish scholar and printer), suggesting that his six-year-old son could learn Latin simply by hearing it spoken: 'and this is the way in which once upon a time Roman youth was taught' (et sic olim Romana iuventus instituebatur). He mentioned the case of a four-year-old boy ('puer quadrimulus') whose father 'taught his young child Latin, the same way which ordinary people use for the vernacular' (filium tenellum Latine docuit, haud aliter atque vulgus hominum factitat in idiomate vernaculo).[30]

Also in the fourth decade of the sixteenth century, we read that Henri (1528–98) and Robert (1530–70) Estienne grew up in similar circumstances, in the household of the famous humanist and printer Robert Estienne the elder. Latin was the lingua franca not only among the ten learned proofreaders (who had different mother tongues), but also among the servants and all the members of the family, so that Henri and Robert heard only the Latin language used, 'since, once the first foundations were established, we started chattering in it' (ex quo iactis primis fundamentis balbutire in ea coeperamus).[31]

Nevertheless, for Henri Estienne also, Latin, however at ease with it he had been since early childhood, was not considered a mother tongue. In his *De Lipsii Latinitate* he observes that, after writing in French about the French language, he now thought he was facing a much more difficult task, 'writing about the Latin language, foreign to me, not about the vernacular' (de Latina lingua, mihi peregrina, non de vernacula, scribens).[32] In spite of his early acquisition of Latin, to him it still felt like a foreign, not a native, language.

## 3.4. Hebrew
A different case is that of Hebrew.[33] Despite some striking but

superficial analogies, this case is quite separate from the few isolated and highly artificial examples already mentioned of Latin acquired by young children in the Renaissance[34] and different, too, from the attempts to revitalize Irish between the nineteenth and the twentieth centuries.[35] What makes the revival of Hebrew unique is its success. Since I am not a Hebraist, I shall make only a few comments, based on secondary literature.

It is generally assumed that Hebrew ceased to be a spoken language in about the second century of the Common Era, replaced in ordinary usage by Aramaic. As a written language Hebrew remained alive, being the sacred language of the Bible, and continued to be used in the Mishna, the compilation of the oral law, and other writings. For everyday life, Jews in the Diaspora used the local vernaculars (sometimes in forms called 'Jewish languages'). Particularly important were Yiddish (based on Medieval German, used by the Ashkenazi communities in eastern Europe), and Ladino (based on fifteenth-century Spanish, used by the Sephardic communities in North Africa, the Middle East, and the Balkans).

Hebrew was used in scholarship, in an uninterrupted tradition, throughout Late Antiquity, the Middle Ages, and the Early Modern and Modern periods – not only in writing but also, for instance, in sermons prepared for oral delivery. We could compare it to Latin, in the sense that it was not 'dead'; it was still employed, but as a literary language, not as a mother tongue; it was a 'High' rather than a 'Low' variety, in the context of diglossia.[36]

In 1881 Tsar Alexander II was assassinated. He was succeeded by Alexander III, who was extremely reactionary and anti-Semitic, and a wave of pogroms forced the emigration of many Russian Jews. In 1881 Ben-Yehuda, considered the founder of modern Hebrew, moved to Palestine and started work on his monumental Hebrew dictionary. Ben-Yehuda was born Eliezer Yitzhak Perelman in Lithuania in 1858.[37] He was a native speaker of Yiddish, and, according to his biographers, as a child he is unlikely to have had more than a rudimentary knowledge of Russian and Lithuanian. He learnt to read Hebrew fluently. Later, he studied modern languages (French and German, as well as Russian) and joined the Russian populist revolutionary movement, the Narodniki. At the time of the Russo-Turkish war (1877–8) he enthusiastically adopted the ideals that, for the Balkans as for the rest of Europe, linked the aspiration to national independence with the notion that language provided the main identifying character of peoples. Ben-Yehuda came to believe in the ideal of a Jewish national state in Palestine, based on a generalized use of the Hebrew language.

In Palestine the linguistic situation was complex.[38] In the period 1882–1914 the Jewish population grew from 24,000 to 85,000. The immigrants spoke mainly Yiddish or Ladino and, since the two languages were reciprocally unintelligible, Hebrew was occasionally employed as a lingua franca ('market Hebrew').[39] Its use grew steadily, and Ben-Yehuda became one of its most active upholders. By 1914 it seems that Hebrew was used by 40 per cent of the Jewish population.

As early as 1878–9 Ben-Yehuda wrote for Peretz Smolenskin's journal *Ha-Shahar* an article with the title 'A Burning Question' (the editor changed it to 'An Important Question,' *She'elah Nikhbadah*), in which he argued for a revival of written (*tehiyyat ha-lashon*) rather than spoken Hebrew (*tehiyyat ha-dibbur*). The latter idea emerged in 1879 and 1880.[40] It was, in fact, a controversial suggestion. The more traditional religious elements felt that using Hebrew for everyday dealings was a defilement of the Holy Tongue. Also, there were other languages that struggled to become the dominant tongue in Palestine: Yiddish, French, and even German. Heated discussions about the choice of a national language took place in 1913 and are designated as the 'language war.'

All these rivals had an advantage over Hebrew insofar as they were proper mother tongues, employed by native speakers. This point is well taken in a sentence attributed to the famous poet Bialik: 'Yidish redt zich, hebreyish darf man reydn' (Yiddish speaks itself, Hebrew has to be spoken).[41] Besides, Yiddish was characteristically a Jewish language, one of the Jewish vernaculars. That the same was true of modern Hebrew could not be taken for granted. In fact, Nathan Birnbaum had observed as early as 1909 that by becoming a historical-national language Hebrew was becoming less Jewish,[42] and an Israeli linguist, Uzzi Ornan, argued explicitly that a 'Jewish language' is one that Jews speak among themselves and is different from the one used outside the home and the neighbourhood, whereas Hebrew in Israel is a 'state language,' that is, from this viewpoint, a language of the gentiles, not a Jewish language.[43] It was the very success of Hebrew that, in this sense, changed its nature. In 1989 in Israel there were celebrations for the 100th anniversary of the revival of the language – with reference to the foundation in 1889 of the 'Hebrew Language Committee,' which was to become in 1953 the 'Language Academy.'[44]

The current literature on the revival of Hebrew stresses two elements in particular, for both of which Ben-Yehuda's impulse was crucial. One was the insistence on teaching Hebrew through Hebrew. In 1883 Nissim Bechar, principal of the Torah U-Melakha School for boys of the Alliance Israélite Universelle in Jerusalem, offered Ben-Yehuda a teaching post, which he accepted on condition that he be allowed to teach in Hebrew. This was the 'Berlitz,' 'direct,' or 'natural' method. Ben-Yehuda was able to teach for only three months,[45] but use of the direct method spread. The direct method, however, was always intended to be an effective technique to teach a foreign or second language, never to produce native speakers.

This is, in fact, the second element: the struggle to extend teaching Hebrew through Hebrew to children of an ever lower age, until one reached children so small that effectively they were acquiring Hebrew as their first language (or on a par with another first language that might be used at home). In 1894 the foundations for the first kindergarten were laid; in 1896 three-year-old children were admitted; and finally, in 1898 the first Hebrew kindergarten was opened in Rishon Le-Zion, followed by one in Jerusalem in 1903 and others elsewhere from 1904.[46]

It is in this context that we may expect to find the first 'native speakers' of Hebrew. The first generation of normal native speakers of Hebrew, acquiring the language not only in the kindergarten but also at home, consisted of the children born in the first ten years of the twentieth century, whose parents had gone to Hebrew schools and were using the language confidently and fluently (although not as native speakers, since it was not their first or only language).[47]

There is also a slightly different account, which has gained wide popularity. The birth of the first native speaker of Hebrew can be pinpointed with absolute precision: he was the son of Ben-Yehuda, Ben-Zion (later called Ittamar Ben-Avi), who died in America in 1943. He was born on 31 July 1882,[48] and his father had decided that he was to become a Hebrew native speaker and was to hear only Hebrew around him. The problem was that his mother, Eliezer's first wife, Deborah Jonas, was a speaker of Yiddish and Russian, not of Hebrew, and Ben-Yehuda himself at the time found it difficult to talk about ordinary things in Hebrew. He once became furious with his wife when he overheard her singing lullabies to their son in her native Russian – after which, at the late age of four, the child miraculously started to speak, and his first sentences were in Hebrew, which caused a sensation among the neighbours, who had feared he would grow up deaf and dumb.[49]

Notwithstanding these painful beginnings and the fact that it was often described as a 'father's tongue' (because fathers could answer children coming home from school or kindergarten, in their language, while mothers, as is common in immigrant societies, had to learn it from their children), modern Hebrew went on to become a real mother tongue, spoken by native speakers, and one of the great success stories in modern sociolinguistics. The revival of Hebrew was even described by Edward Ullendorff as 'one of the most genuinely creative accomplishments of our time.'[50]

### 3.5. *Italian*

There are some questions concerning the mother tongue that seem to be even more disturbing for Italian than for other languages. Usually, if you are looking for a native speaker of Italian or for someone whose mother tongue is Italian, you are asking for an 'authoritative,' 'reliable,' 'competent' informant who may be able to help you to answer certain questions, such as: does one say *ca*[s]*a* or *ca*[z]*a* for 'house'? Does one say *arancia* or *arancio* for 'orange'? Does one say *li si vede* or *li si vedono* for 'one can see them'? But this is the sort of question on which the more competent you are as a native speaker, the less likely you are to offer straightforward answers.

In the history of Italian culture, the dialect vs standard diglossia is additional to the traditional diglossia we find existing in Europe since the Middle Ages between Latin and the vernacular. Until the nineteenth century, educated people had access to three different languages: first, one of the dialects, that is, their mother tongue, which might or might not have a written tradition as well, such as Venetian, Milanese, Neapolitan, and so on; second, the standard language, that is, the literary language, or the national language, based on the literary form of fourteenth-century Tuscan, as codified in the sixteenth century (and also available in other varieties influenced by regional features and by Latin); and third, Latin itself. Of these, only the first, that is, the dialect (originally more appropriately designated as a 'vernacular'), could be considered a mother tongue, of which people were native speakers. The second and third were literary languages, acquired through literacy, when one learnt to read and write.

The peculiar nature of Italian as a literary language rather than a mother tongue was, in fact, widely recognized from the start. Pietro Bembo, who codified the literary language, observed, through his brother Carlo, in the *Prose della volgar lingua* (1525), that 'in our own time being born Florentine is not very useful for writing good Florentine' (l'essere a questi tempi nato fiorentino, a ben volere fiorentino scrivere, non sia di molto vantaggio),[51] which is as good a way as any of marking the distinction between mother tongue and literary language. Three centuries later, Alessandro Manzoni pointed out that 'there is in Italy no language that is, as they say, sucked with the mother's milk, used, understood by everyone, the language, in other words, of those who only have one language, and which therefore can be called the Italians' very own native language and can in this sense properly be termed the Italian language' (non c'è in Italia una lingua la qual sia da tutti succhiata, come si dice, col latte, adoperata, intesa da tutti, la lingua insomma di quelli che ne intendono una sola, la quale, per conseguenza, si possa chiamar lingua propria e nativa di tutti gl'italiani, la quale si possa in questo senso denominar lingua italiana).[52]

There is an interesting chronological parallel in the discussions concerning Italian and Hebrew that took place during the last thirty years of the nineteenth century. As explained earlier, as soon as Ben-Yehuda arrived in Palestine in 1881, he started work on his formidable enterprise, *Millon ha-lashon ha-ivrit ha-yeshanah ve-hadashah (A Complete Dictionary of Ancient and Modern Hebrew*, also with a Latin title, *Thesaurus totius hebraitatis et veteris et recentioris*), published in seventeen volumes between 1908 and 1959.

This was meant to be a full dictionary destined for the Jewish nation, which, Ben-Yehuda hoped, was to adopt Hebrew as its ordinary language. In the introductory comments in the first volume, signed by the publisher (Prof. G. Langenscheidt) and presumably written or approved by the author, reference is made to 'resuscitating the Hebrew language, and making it a popular vehicle of everyday speech ... reinstating Hebrew as a colloquial medium, as the family language and mother-tongue of the growing generation.'[53]

Italian already could boast an authoritative dictionary, in fact, the first important vernacular dictionary among the nations of Europe, the *Vocabolario degli Accademici della Crusca* of 1612, later enlarged and reprinted in the following centuries. It was a puristic dictionary of a literary language, however, and had a rather remote link with everyday speech. Manzoni, the greatest Italian writer of the nineteenth century, wrote in his *Marzo 1821* (lines 31–2), a patriotic poem probably composed in 1821 but published much later in 1848, that Italy was 'One in arms, language, altar, / memories, blood and heart' (Una d'arme, di lingua, d'altare, / Di memorie, di sangue e di cor).[54] Once political unification had been achieved, he felt more and more strongly that the linguistic unity, which was supposed to be the basis for the creation of an Italian nation-state, ought to be finally realized, at least a posteriori. After a long and complex intellectual journey, Manzoni had reached the conclusion that the mother tongue of the new state was to be the ordinary language of the educated middle classes in Florence. Italians were to become native speakers of that idiom. It would be a contribution towards remedying the situation described by Massimo D'Azeglio: 'unfortunately, while Italy has been created, Italians are not being created' (pur troppo s'è fatta l'Italia, ma non si fanno gli Italiani).[55] Manzoni's solution was to produce a dictionary of such a language – the *Novo vocabolario della lingua italiana secondo l'uso di Firenze*, which was published between 1870 and 1897.[56] However interesting this dictionary is for us, and whatever its merits (including provoking Ascoli's memorable critical intervention, the *Proemio*),[57] it certainly did not contribute to the emergence of Italian native speakers. According to Tullio De Mauro, in a recent lecture given at the Italian Department of University College London, the desire for the mother tongue was so desperate that one of the participants in the discussions raging at the time went so far as to suggest that Italian men ought to go to Tuscany to look for a wife, so that their children would naturally grow up as native speakers of Tuscan.

Concerning the native speakers of Italian, the commonly held view is that they started appearing after 1950, owing to the general diffusion of television, which for the first time in Italian history made spoken Italian familiar to everyone in the country. Of course, even during the first half of the twentieth century, in middle-class families, adults, who themselves were mainly native speakers of a dialect, in order to improve their children's prospects for the future tended to speak Italian with them. Usually, however, these children heard the dialect spoken around them in the family and, in turn, used it outside the home. It is only during the second half of the century that a sizeable part of the population started using only or mainly Italian, and we therefore find children who can be described as native speakers of Italian rather than dialect.

Attempting to distinguish between native speakers and native-like speakers who are, in fact, non-native, on the basis of objective tests, turns out to be more problematic than expected. About fifteen years ago René Coppieters published in *Language* an article in which he presented his findings about the difference in competence between native and near-native speakers of French, on the basis of extensive interviews. The two groups appeared to be indistinguishable at the level of language use and proficiency, but strikingly different at the level of underlying grammar. This fact was apparent from their comments concerning their intuitions about certain grammatical structures (sentences with third-person pronouns, pre- and postnominal adjectives, imperfect and passé composé, prepositions, secondary clauses, articles). Concerning the first point, he gives, for instance, sentences such as

(1) Qui est Victor Hugo? *Il/√C'est un grand écrivain du XIXème siècle.
(2) Je connais cette statue, √elle/√c'est le symbole de la paix.
(3) Tu vois ce type-là, *il/√c'est l'idiot qui a renversé mon verre.[58]

The natives agreed about grammaticality, as indicated by asterisks and ticks in our examples, while the non-natives, although producing correct sentences in their usage, were unable to reject firmly the ungrammatical ones or, in the case of (2), to recognize that, although both alternatives are grammatical, only *elle* refers directly to *statue*. According to Sascha W. Felix,[59] this contrast, between usage on the one hand, and judgments of acceptability on the other, depends on the fact that language acquisition (which characterizes native speakers) is based on a language-specific faculty, while language learning (taking place after puberty) relies on a general problem-solving ability.

A recent interesting study by Paolo Acquaviva, who teaches Italian linguistics in Dublin, shows that it is helpful, indeed necessary, to distinguish what native speakers 'do' from what they 'know.' Consider, for example, the following sentences:

(4) non mi resta che concludere ...
(5) i signori viaggiatori sono pregati recarsi ...
(6) non mi resta che di concludere ...
(7) i signori viaggiatori sono pregati di recarsi ...[60]

Someone who has a good command of Italian, but is not a native speaker, tends to look at the two pairs (4/6) and (5/7) as being equivalent, both illustrating the possibility of inserting or omitting a *di* between the main verb and the dependent infinitive in Italian. Native speakers, however, on the basis of their internalized grammar, have the intuition that (4/6) are legitimate, superficial variations of the same structure; whereas (5) is a conventional, abbreviated formula, used as such in a sort of railway-announcement shorthand but unacceptable as an instance of the grammatical structure represented by (7). This is confirmed by the fact that in structures like (4/6) one can vary the verb and obtain grammatical results (*desidero*, *preferisco*, etc., *concludere* or *di concludere*), whereas in structures like (5/7) *sono sospettati*, *accusati*, etc., *recarsi* cannot be accepted without the *di*.

I noticed a comparable example in a German-speaking village in the Alto Adige (the Italian South Tyrol), where the locals are native speakers of a Bavarian dialect. Among the notices placed along the mountain roads by the civic administration one finds examples such as *Divieto (di) caccia/raccolta funghi/sosta*, with or without *di*, and *vietata (la) caccia/raccolta funghi/sosta*, with or without the *la*. The people responsible, who are not native speakers of Italian, have apparently extrapolated a rule that allows insertion or omission of the preposition *di*, or the appropriate article, according to the space available. One result is that, on the basis of *divieto (di) scarico* and *vietato (lo) scarico*, they also produced *divieto lo scarico*, clearly impossible for a native speaker of Italian. As we can see, both *divieto lo scarico* and *i signori viaggiatori sono pregati recarsi ...* exist in real life, but we judge them differently in terms of acceptability on the basis of our intuitions as native speakers.

Similarly, we ought to be able to investigate the distinction between Italians who are native speakers of Italian, and those who are native speakers of a dialect, on the basis of their judgments of grammaticality. For instance, we can compare the following four sentences, which I quote from Acquaviva:

(8)  Non sto dicendo che Gianni deve rinunciare al suo incarico.
(9)  Non sto dicendo che Gianni debba rinunciare al suo incarico.
(10)  Non sto dicendo che Gianni deve rinunciare a niente.
(11)  Non sto dicendo che Gianni debba rinunciare a niente.[61]

For some speakers of Italian, sentence (10) is ungrammatical, because the association of *non* and *niente* makes the use of the subjunctive compulsory. For other speakers (10) is grammatical, and the relation between (10) and (11) is identical to that between (8) and (9), that is, the usual relation between (a) an indicative that is more colloquial or approximates a sort of indirect free style, preserving the indicative of direct speech reporting: 'Non sto dicendo: "Gianni deve rinunciare al suo incarico,"' and (b) a subjunctive that is more literary and exhibits the mood expected in a secondary clause. Those who are not aware of any difference between the first pair and the second seem to have learnt to use the subjunctive as they might have done in a second language, that is, without recourse to those spontaneous and unselfconscious intuitions characteristic of the natives. In this sense they are not native speakers of Italian.

If I compare the situation in Venetian, a northern Italian dialect of which I am a native speaker, I find that it is even more clear-cut:

(10a)  No stago dizendo che Nane gabia da far de manco de gnente

is fully grammatical, while

(11a)  No stago dizendo che Nane ga da far de manco de gnente

is ungrammatical. Perhaps I should say it is ungrammatical as an ordinary, unmarked sentence; if I consider it a marked sentence, conveying a special connotation, or an example of indirect free style, as above, then I have to consider it acceptable.

Acquaviva is, of course, fully aware of the complexity of the situation. He observes that we obviously accept that native speakers of different languages, such as Italian and French, have different competences, that is, different internalized grammars, different mother tongues. It is likely that the same reasoning applies to native speakers of Italian and a northern Italian dialect, which might lead us to distinguish also native speakers of popular Italian from those of standard Italian. One would need to add, first, that present-day dialect speakers may hide under a grammar that on the surface seems to belong to the dialect, a competence that is indistinguishable from that of a monolingual speaker of Italian; and second, that native competence may depend on regional (diatopic) or social (diastratic) variation, but not on differences in subject matter, levels of formality, emotional attitude, and so on (diaphasic variation): it would be, according to Acquaviva, 'like postulating native speakers of pompous Italian who are non native speakers of informal Italian.'[62] One obviously has to agree, however tempting the hypothesis may be, that one does occasionally meet speakers whose pomposity is native.

To return to our examples of the subjunctive, I consider myself a native speaker of Italian as well as of Venetian. This adds a further dimension to my intuition concerning (10), *Non sto dicendo che Gianni deve rinunciare a niente*. On the one hand, it seems to me to carry a connotation of popular Italian, replacing the expected subjunctive with an indicative. On the other, since the Venetian dialect would require here the subjunctive, and a Venetian speaker of popular Italian might be inclined to transfer into Italian the mood used in the dialect, the indicative might represent a hyper-correct form, that is, a structure at one further remove from the dialect, rather than calqued on it. Although my intuition seems fairly clear as far as my own usage is concerned, it becomes less straightforward if I am trying to evaluate another speaker's sentence.

## 4. *Literary Language*

In the final section of this chapter I should like to mention an aspect that is perhaps even less tractable, in the context of linguistics, than those I have mentioned up to now.

Italian is an instance of a well-known language, the vehicle of a famous literature extending over eight centuries, with writers of world stature, such as Dante, Petrarch, Boccaccio, Ariosto, Tasso, Leopardi, Manzoni, but it is also a language that, it could be said, until fairly recently had no native speakers and was no one's mother tongue. Before concluding, we should ask whether this characteristic is, in fact, so surprising and exceptional. The question can be considered from a historical and comparative angle and from a more theoretical point of view with reference to the language of poetry.

Concerning the first angle, we have already examined the case of Latin in the Middle Ages and in the Renaissance and that of Hebrew from the third century C.E. to the end of the nineteenth century. A diglossic situation, however, in which the mother tongue and the literary medium are quite distinct (either because they are different varieties of the same language or because they are different languages), seems to be prevalent in recorded history throughout the world; and the modern European situation, in which a nation-state tends to favour the use of the same idiom for literary expression and for everyday communication among the whole population, appears to be the exception rather than the norm. One often gets the impression that nineteenth- and twentieth-century scholarship has projected onto previous centuries an evaluation of the mother tongue that is, in fact, more appropriate to Romantic culture and the formation of Nationalism.

It is well known that many authors of classical antiquity, such as Livius Andronicus, Plautus, Seneca, Augustine, were not native speakers of Latin, and it seems legitimate to ask ourselves whether, for instance, Virgil or Catullus did not have the opportunity, when they were children in Mantua or Verona, to speak with local children, and, if they did, one wonders what languages they used.

In recent years people have looked with growing interest at writers who use in their works 'another' language, different from their mother tongue. A brilliant example is Giorgio Pressburger, one of the most striking contemporary Italian writers, who was born in Hungary, speaks many languages, and learnt Italian only as an adult. He discussed this topic a few years ago in a paper I heard, in Italian, in his native Budapest (where he is now director of the Italian Cultural Institute),[63] and again in a fascinating lecture, in English, held at University College London on 25 November 1999, entitled 'Far from the Mother Tongue.' Pressburger listed authors who wrote in 'another' language (or in a language 'other'), from Conrad to Svevo, to Canetti, to Beckett, to Nabokov, to the panoply of anglophone and francophone writers who did not grow up as native speakers of English or French. My own lack of expertise precludes my discussing the new literature produced in Australia, the United States, and Canada by Italian immigrants and that produced in Italy by writers recently immigrated from North Africa.

The final point concerns the second topic mentioned above, the language of poetry. One of the most widely held assumptions among our colleagues is that one can write poetry, and (more relevantly for those of us who teach in a modern language department) one can write seriously about poetry, only if one is dealing with the mother tongue. I think we can all sympathize with the feeling of inadequacy that lies behind this position, since we are constantly made aware of the insufficiency of our understanding.

If it is any consolation, however, we should reflect that it is perhaps a question of degree. I am not convinced that an Italian native speaker is better qualified than an English Dantist to understand *The Divine Comedy* or that a native speaker of English is better suited than an Italian Shakespeare scholar to understand *Hamlet*. The real difficulty seems to lie not in the native language nor in the control we have of the idiom we use for everyday communication (be it a first or a second language) but rather in the nature of poetry. Here, we are touching something that concerns an essential quality of language, but in a sense that escapes the technical tools we employ as linguists. From this viewpoint no one is a native speaker of the language of poetry. We are reminded of Marina Tsvetaeva's words, made famous by Paul Celan: 'All poets are Jews.' In the original, visiting Prague's ancient ghetto, Tsvetaeva says: 'In this most Christian of worlds / Poets – Jews.' As John Felstiner observes in his book about Celan, the Russian *Poety – zhidy*, in fact, uses the derogatory designation for Jews: 'all poets are Yids.'[64] The language of poetry is a language of outsiders, of strangers.[65]

One is struck by the extraordinary energy of poetry written in dialect in modern Italy and by how 'un-dialectal' it is.[66] It is often written by poets who are not even 'native speakers' of the dialect in a technical sense but have created their own poetic idiom, which reaches deeper than the regions accessed by ordinary language, the 'language that calls mum or dad' (lingua che chiami mamma o babbo), in Dante's words (*Inferno*, 32, 9). It reaches deeper, because they are poets, using the language of poetry, not because they are native speakers using their mother tongues. I should like to end with a quotation from the Triestine poet, Virgilio Giotti, who, as Pier Paolo Pasolini relates,[67] once was horrified at being asked whether he used his dialect for everyday communication: certainly not, he answered, dialect is the language of poetry (la lingua della poesia).

NOTES

1  Leonard Bloomfield, *Language* (New York: Holt, 1933), 43.

2  Noam Chomsky, *Syntactic Structures* (The Hague: Mouton, 1957), 13; see also 49–50.

3  Florian Coulmas, ed., *A Festschrift for the Native Speaker* (The Hague: Mouton, 1981); Thomas M. Paikeday, *The Native Speaker Is Dead! An Informal Discussion on Linguistic Myth with Noam Chomsky and Other Linguists, Philosophers, Psychologists, and Lexicographers* (Toronto: Paikeday, 1985); Alan Davies, *The Native Speaker in Applied Linguistics* (Edinburgh: Edinburgh University Press, 1991); Rajendra Singh, ed., *The Native Speaker: Multilingual Perspectives* (New Delhi: Sage, 1998).

4  Giulio Lepschy and Helena Sanson, '"(Non-)Native Speakers" and "(M)Other Tongues,"' *Anglistica* 3:1 (1999), 79–92; Giulio Lepschy and Helena Sanson, 'Native Speaker,' in *Reflexivity: Critical Themes in the Italian Cultural Tradition. Essays by Members of the Department of Italian at University College London*, ed. Prue Shaw and John Took (Ravenna: Longo, 2000), 119–29.

5  'Native Irish' is, of course, a traditional designation; see, for instance, several tracts of the early nineteenth century by Christopher Anderson, with titles such as *Memorial on behalf of the Native Irish, with a view to their improvement in moral and religious knowledge through the medium of their own language* (London: Gale, Curtis & Fenner, 1815); *Historical Sketches of the Ancient Native Irish and their Descendants; Illustrative of their past and present state with regard to Literature, Education, and Oral Instruction* (Edinburgh: Oliver & Boyd, 1828); *Ireland, But Still Without the Ministry of the Word in her Own Native Language* (Edinburgh: Oliver & Boyd, 1835).

6  David Crystal has pointed out to me, in personal correspondence, that the OED, *s.v. speaker*, as a second element (§7), gives *English speaker* in a quote from Whitney (1875), and combinations of *native* with *language* (Hawes, 1509), *tongue* (Shelley, 1817), *speech* (Skeat, 1887), apart from individual names of languages, such as *native English* (Shakespeare, 1593). Crystal also pointed out that *natural* seems to have been common, before *native* came along. (In fact, the entries for *native* and *natural* in the OED show that they were often interchangeable.) *Natural language* is quoted from Wilkins, 1668 ('no one Language is natural to mankind'), and Monboddo, 1774, apart from the frequent collocations in which it is contrasted with *artificial language* in the second half of the nineteenth century. With reference to national origins, we

find 'true naturall Englishmen' (1556), 'naturall Scottismen' (1572), 'Good and naturall English words' (1579), 'a natural Venetian' (1624), and so on, and specifically with reference to languages: 'All the Candians speaking Italian as well as their naturall Greek tongue' (Moryson, 1617); 'The Sclavonians ... made suit unto the Pope to have the publick Service in their natural Tongue' (Heylin, 1657–61).

7  Christopher M. Hutton, *Linguistics and the Third Reich: Mother-Tongue Fascism, Race, and the Science of Language* (London: Routledge, 1999).

8  Leo Weisgerber, *Muttersprache und Geistesbildung* (Göttingen: Vandenhoeck & Ruprecht, 1929), followed by *Die volkhaften Kräfte der Muttersprache* (Frankfurt: Diesterweg, 1938; I have consulted the British Library copy of the third edition of 1943).

9  See Georg Schmidt-Rohr, *Die Sprache als Bildnerin der Völker: Eine Wesens- und Lebenskunde der Volkstümer* (Jena: Diederichs, 1932), promptly republished in 1933 with a preface celebrating Hitler's victory and with a new title: *Mutter Sprache: Von Amt der Sprache bei der Volkwerdung* (Jena: Diederichs, 1933).

10  Otto Behagel, 'Lingua Materna,' *Zeitschrift für französische Sprache und Literatur*, Suppl. 13 (1929) [Festschrift Wilhelm Adolf Baehrens], 13–15.

11  Leo Weisgerber, 'Ist *Muttersprache* eine Germanische oder eine Romanische Wortprägung?' *PBB* [Hermann Paul and Wilhelm Braune's *Beiträge zur Geschichte der deutschen Sprache und Literatur*] 62 (1938), 428–37.

12  *PL* [*Patrologia Latina*], 163, col. 1084.

13  Leo Spitzer, 'Muttersprache und Muttererziehung,' in his *Essays in Historical Semantics* (New York: Vanni, 1948), 15–65. See also the review by J[akob] J[ud], *Vox Romanica* 11 (1950), 245–8.

14  Helena Sanson, in her work for her dissertation, has traced several others, mostly from speakers of French, English, and Italian vernaculars, rather than German; see, for instance, *materna lingua* (1123–8) in the *Consuetudines Canonicorum Regularium* from Springiersbach Klosterrath, *CCCM* [*Corpus Christianorum. Continuatio Mediaevalis*], vol. 48, ed. Stephanus Weinfurter (Turnhout: Brepols, 1978), 25; *materno sermone* in Guibert de Nogent, 1110 and 1124 (*PL* 156, cols. 699 and 913); *materna lingua* in the *Vita S. Odonis* (*PL*, 133, col. 944), in the *Vita Dunstani* (*PL*, 159, col. 792), in the *Vita S. Norberti* (*PL*, 170, col. 1273), in an *Epistola* of 1148 of Wibaldus of Corvey (*PL*, 189, col. 1206), in Johannes Beleth (d. 1182), *CCCM*, vol. 41-A, ed. Heribertus Douteil (Turnhout: Brepols, 1976), 218.

15  See Karl Heisig, 'Muttersprache,' *Zeitschrift für Mundartforschung* 22 (1954), 144–74; Jean Batany, 'L'amère maternité du français médiéval,' *Langue française* 54 (1982), 29–39; and references in Lepschy and Sanson, '"(Non-)Native Speakers,"' n. 35.

16  Heymann Steinthal, 'Von der Liebe zur Muttersprache,' in his *Gesammelte kleine Schriften*, vol. 1 (Berlin: Dümmlers, 1880), 97–107.

17  Benedetto Varchi, *L'Hercolano*, ed. Antonio Sorella (Pescara: Libreria dell'Università Editrice, 1995), 647.

18  *Il nuovo etimologico: DELI – Dizionario etimologico della lingua italiana*, by Manlio Cortelazzo and Paolo Zolli, 2nd ed. in one volume, ed. Manlio Cortelazzo and Michele A. Cortelazzo (Bologna: Zanichelli, 1999), 878. Helena Sanson has identified an even earlier one, for *madre lingua*, from the *Vocabolista Bolognese* (1660) by Giovanni Antonio Bumaldi (pseudonym of Ovidio Montalbani).

19  Philip Larkin, 'Annus Mirabilis,' in his *Collected Poems* (London: Faber and Faber, 1988), 167.

20  Friedrich Nietzsche, *Die fröhliche Wissenschaft*, III, 108 (Chemnitz: Schmeitzner, 1882), 137.

21  Roland Barthes, 'La mort de l'auteur,' in his *Essais critiques IV: Le bruissement de la langue* (Paris: Seuil, 1984), 61–8.

22  Carlo Tagliavini, *Introduzione alla glottologia*, vol. 1 (Bologna: Pàtron, 1963), 443.

23  Daniel Nettle, Suzanne Romaine, *Vanishing Voices: The Extinction of the World's Languages* (Oxford: Oxford University Press, 2000).

24  David Crystal, *Language Death* (Cambridge: Cambridge University Press, 2000).

25  See the contributions by Henri François Muller (1921), Ferdinand Lot (1931), Dag Norberg (1966), Michael Richter (1983), Marc van Uytfanghe (1983), and Brian Stock, *The Implications of Literacy: Written Language and Models of Interpretation in the Eleventh and Twelfth Centuries* (Princeton: Princeton University Press, 1983); Yvonne Cazal, *La voix du peuple – Verbum Dei: Le bilinguisme Latin – Langue vulgaire au Moyen Âge* (Geneva: Droz, 1998).

26  Ferdinand Brunot, *Histoire de la langue française des origines à 1900*, tome II, *Le seizième siècle* (Paris: Colin, 1906), 8, mentions Montaigne and Henri Estienne and comments: 'It might seem that we have here an exceptional case. Not at all.' (Il semble qu'on soit ici en présence d'un cas exceptionnel. Nullement.) The means may have varied, but the aims were widely shared. See, how-

ever, the sceptical considerations by Roger Trinquet, *La Jeunesse de Montaigne: Ses origines familiales, son enfance et ses études* (Paris: Nizet, 1972), 198.

27 In Michel de Montaigne, *Oeuvres complètes*, ed. Albert Thibaudet and Maurice Rat (Paris: Gallimard, 1962), 172–3.

28 Trinquet, *La Jeunesse*, 238–40.

29 Erasmus, *Declamatio de pueris statim ac liberaliter instituendis*, ed. Jean-Claude Margolin (Geneva: Droz, 1966), 421, 423, 445.

30 Nicolas Clénard, *Correspondance*, ed. Alphonse Roersch, vol. 1 (Brussels: Palais des Académies, 1940), 62–4.

31 Henri Estienne, letter prefaced to Auli Gellii *Noctes Atticae* (Paris: [H. Estienne], 1585), 12–13.

32 Henri Estienne, *De Lipsii Latinitate* (Frankfurt: n.p., 1595), 12–13.

33 I am grateful to Joanna Weinberg for her comments and suggestions about this section.

34 I am grateful to Vivian Salmon, who pointed out to me the case of the English Hebraist Hugh Broughton (1549–1612). He undertook the education of Rowland Cotton by seeing to it that only Hebrew was used with the child, who was later to relate 'that his Mother would sometimes be ready to weep, when he came to do his Duty to her, or to ask any thing from her, and must not speak to her in English, so that she might have conferred with him, and talked to him again' (preface by John Lightfoot to Hugh Broughton, *Works* (London: Ekins, 1662), signature b). See Vivian Salmon, *Language and Society in Early Modern England: Selected Essays 1981–1994*, ed. Konrad Koerner (Amsterdam: Benjamins, 1996), 181–2.

35 See Sue Wright, ed., *Language and the State: Revitalization and Revival in Israel and Eire* (Clevedon: Multilingual Matters, 1996).

36 On the 'survival' of Hebrew see William Chomsky, *Hebrew: The Eternal Language* (Philadelphia: Jewish Publication Society of America, 1958), particularly chaps 11 ('Did Hebrew Ever Die?') and 12 ('The Struggle for Revival'). Chomsky states that 'fluency in the employment of spoken Hebrew did not die out' (217); '[t]he fact of the matter is that Hebrew never died' (227), and he quotes evidence for the use of Hebrew in speech, including the assertion of Azariah de' Rossi, the Italian sixteenth-century scholar: 'Though we are conversant with the Italian language, the numerous members of the intellectual class of our people meditate, speak and write in the Holy Tongue' (219); Azariah de' Rossi's work has recently appeared in English translation with introduction and annotations by Joanna Weinberg: *The Light of the Eyes* (New Haven and London: Yale Uni-

versity Press, 2001). See also Angel Sáenz-Badillos, *A History of the Hebrew Language*, trans. John Elwolde (Cambridge: Cambridge University Press, 1993), particularly chaps 8:2, 8:3. On linguistic thought in the Hebrew tradition, see Raphael Loewe, 'Hebrew Linguistics,' in *History of Linguistics*, vol. 1: *The Eastern Traditions of Linguistics*, ed. Giulio Lepschy (London: Longman, 1994), 97–163, particularly the section 'The hand maiden of nineteenth-century nationalism,' 135–8.

37  Concerning Ben-Yehuda, see his autobiography, originally published in Hebrew in the journal *Ha-Toren*, 1917–18, and in English translation by Takamitsu Muraoka, *A Dream Come True* (Boulder: Westview Press, 1993); Jack Fellman, *The Revival of a Classical Tongue: Eliezer Ben-Yehuda and the Modern Hebrew Language* (The Hague: Mouton, 1973); Eisig Silberschlag, ed., *Eliezer Ben-Yehuda: A Symposium in Oxford* (Oxford: Oxford Centre for Postgraduate Hebrew Studies, 1981).

38  Roberto Bachi, 'A Statistical Analysis of the Revival of Hebrew in Israel,' *Scripta Hierosolymitana: Publications of the Hebrew University, Jerusalem* 3 (1956), 179–247; T.V. Parfitt, 'The Use of Hebrew in Palestine, 1800–1882,' *Journal of Semitic Studies* 17:2 (1972), 237–52; Bernard Spolsky and Robert L. Cooper, *The Languages of Jerusalem* (Oxford: Clarendon Press, 1991); Bernard Spolsky, 'Language Conflict in Jerusalem – 1880 and 1980,' in *Language Conflict and Language Planning*, ed. Ernst Håkon Jahr (Berlin and New York: Mouton de Gruyter, 1993), 179–92; Edward Ullendorff, 'Hebrew in Mandatary Palestine,' in *Hebrew Studies from Ezra to Ben-Yehuda*, ed. William Horbury (Edinburgh: Edinburgh University Press, 1999), 300–6.

39  George Mandel, *Who Was Ben-Yehuda with in Boulevard Montmartre?* in *Oxford Centre Papers*, vol. 2 (Oxford: Oxford Centre for Postgraduate Hebrew Studies, 1984), 5.

40  George Mandel, 'Why Did Ben-Yehuda Suggest the Revival of Spoken Hebrew?' in *Hebrew in Ashkenaz: A Language in Exile*, ed. Lewis Glinert (New York: Oxford University Press, 1993), 193–207; and 'Resistance to the Study of Hebrew: The Experiences of Peretz Smolenskin and Eliezer Ben-Yehuda,' in Horbury, *Hebrew Studies*, 293–9.

41  Benjamin Harshav, *Language in Time of Revolution* (Berkeley and Los Angeles: University of California Press, 1993), 86.

42  Joshua A. Fishman, 'The Sociology of Jewish Languages from a General Sociolinguistic Point of View,' in *Readings in the Sociology of Jewish Languages*, ed. Joshua A. Fishman (Leiden: Brill, 1985), 7.

43 Uzzi Ornan, 'Hebrew Is Not a Jewish Language,' in Fishman, *Readings*, 22–3.

44 Harshav, *Language*, 84; Moshe Nahir, 'Micro Language Planning and the Revival of Hebrew: A Schematic Framework,' *Language in Society* 27:3 (1998), 335–57 (see 335).

45 Fellman, *Revival*, 117–18.

46 Fellman, *Revival*, 99.

47 Chaim Rabin, *A Short History of the Hebrew Language* (Jerusalem: Publishing Department of the Jewish Agency [1973]), 62–73.

48 Ben-Yehuda, *A Dream*, 105.

49 Fellman, *Revival*, 38–9; he quotes information ('unfortunately somewhat romanticized') from Ittamar's autobiography, *Im Shaḥar Azmantenu* (Jerusalem, 1961). Ben-Yehuda 'would not let the boy listen even to "the chirpings of birds and the neighing of horses, the braying of donkeys and the fluttering of butterflies, because even they are after all foreign tongues, at any rate not Hebrew."' Concerning Ben-Yehuda's problems with Hebrew, however, Fellman reports a personal communication from Yosef Rivlin, who 'noted that, for example, when Ben Yehuda wanted Devora to pour him a cup of coffee with sugar, he was at a loss to communicate words such as "cup," "saucer," "pour," "spoon," and so on, and would say to his wife, in effect: "Take such and such, and do like so, and bring me this and this, and I will drink" (Khi kax, veasi kax, vehavii likax vee shte).'

50 Edward Ullendorff, *The Two Zions: Reminiscences of Jerusalem and Ethiopia* (Oxford: Oxford University Press, 1988), 100.

51 Pietro Bembo, *Prose e rime*, ed. Carlo Dionisotti (Turin: UTET, 1966), 114.

52 Alessandro Manzoni, *Della lingua italiana*, ed. Luigi Poma and Angelo Stella (*Tutte le opere*, vol. 5:1) (Milan: Mondadori, 1974), 11.

53 E. Ben-Yehuda, *Thesaurus totius hebraitatis et veteris et recentioris*, vol. 1 (Schoenberg: Langenscheidt, 1908).

54 Alessandro Manzoni, *Tutte le poesie, 1812–1872*, ed. Gilberto Lonardi (Venice: Marsilio, 1987), 106.

55 On the history of this sentence see Simonetta Soldani, and Gabriele Turi, eds, *Fare gli italiani: Scuola e cultura nell'Italia contemporanea*, vol. 1 (Bologna: il Mulino, 1993), 17.

56 *Novo vocabolario della lingua italiana secondo l'uso di Firenze* (Florence: M. Cellini alla Galileiana, 1870–97), generally known as 'Giorgini-Broglio' from the names of the two main editors, Emilio Broglio and Giovan Battista Giorgini; reprinted, with introduction by Ghino Ghinassi (Florence: Le Lettere, 1979).

57 Graziadio Isaia Ascoli, 'Proemio,' *Archivio glottologico italiano*, 1 (1873), V–XLI. There are several modern editions, for example, in Graziadio Isaia Ascoli, *Scritti sulla questione della lingua*, ed. Corrado Grassi (Turin: Einaudi, 1975).

58 René Coppieters, 'Competence Difference between Native and Near-Native Speakers,' *Language* 63 (1987), 544–73, 555.

59 Sascha W. Felix, *Cognition and Language Growth* (Dordrecht: Foris, 1987).

60 Paolo Acquaviva, 'La grammatica italiana: il lavoro comincia adesso,' *Lingua e stile* 35 (2000), 249–71; see 257–8.

61 See ibid., 265.

62 Acquaviva, 'La grammatica,' 263.

63 Giorgio Pressburger, 'Scrittori in fuga dalla lingua madre,' in *Cultura e società alla fine del secondo millennio: Italia e Ungheria*, ed. Ilona Fried (Budapest: ELTE, 1999), 9–12.

64 John Felstiner, *Paul Celan: Poet, Survivor, Jew* (New Haven and London: Yale University Press, 1995), 197.

65 In her 1932 essay *Poèt i vremja* (*The Poet and Time*) Marina Tsvetaeva wrote: 'Every poet is essentially an *émigré*, even in Russia. *Émigré* from the Kingdom of Heaven and from the earthly paradise of nature.' I am quoting from the English translation by Angela Livingstone in *Art in the Light of Conscience* (London: Bristol Classical Press, 1992), 93; in the original, 'Vsjakij poèt po sushchestvu èmigrant, dazhe v Rossii. Èmigrant Carstva Nebesnogo i zemnogo raja prirody,' *Nesobrannye proizvedenija* (Munich: Fink, 1971), 624.

66 See Hermann W. Haller, ed., *The Hidden Italy: A Bilingual Edition of Italian Dialect Poetry* (Detroit: Wayne State University Press, 1986); Emmanuela Tandello and Diego Zancani, eds, *Italian Dialects and Literature: From the Renaissance to the Present* (London: Institute of Romance Studies, 1996), Supplement 1, *Journal of the Institute of Romance Studies*; Hermann W. Haller, *The Other Italy: The Literary Canon in the Dialect* (Toronto: University of Toronto Press, 1999); Franco Brevini, ed., *La poesia in dialetto: Storia e testi dalle origini al Novecento*, 3 vols (Milan: Mondadori, 1999).

67 Pier Paolo Pasolini, *Passione e ideologia (1948–1958)* (Milan: Garzanti, 1960), 281.

# CHAPTER TWO

# *The Languages of Italy*

In this chapter I should like to deal with the Italian linguistic situation from three points of view – first, linguistic variety in Italy: the standard, the dialects, and the minority languages. Second, how much, by whom, and in what circumstances Italian and dialects are used. Third, language policy: how far the rights of the linguistic minorities are guaranteed by Italian law.

## 1. *Linguistic Variety in Italy*

Concerning the first point (standard, dialects, and minority languages) we need to make some terminological clarifications. Standard Italian is based on literary Florentine of the fourteenth century, as it was codified at the beginning of the sixteenth century (see above, chapter one, section 3.5). It was for centuries a written language, known only to a minority of literate people. It has been estimated that at the moment of national unification in 1860 only 2.5 per cent of the population was able to use Italian.[1] There is a more optimistic evaluation, but even that has not been able to produce a figure higher than 10 per cent.[2] It was only during the second half of the twentieth century that Italian became a spoken language that a majority of Italians are able to use in everyday life as their ordinary medium of communication. They are now able to use Italian, but in fact, as we shall see, they do not always do so.

If this is the situation, how did Italians speak during the 700 years from the fourteenth century to the twentieth? What idiom did they use in speech, colloquially, in the ordinary circumstances of everyday life? The answer is: one of the local dialects.

At one level, this is a straight answer to a straight question. At another level, it is an answer that calls for further questions. The first question concerns the distinction between language and dialect.[3] What is the difference, and how does one know whether an idiom is a language or a dialect? Here, the answer is very simple. From a strictly linguistic viewpoint or, let us say, from the viewpoint of grammatical theory, there is no difference. Or rather, the difference is socio-political, not linguistic. To quote a well-known dictum by Max Weinreich, the Yiddish scholar, 'a language is a dialect which has an army and a navy.' True, perhaps with some provisos. Literary Italian was for centuries a language, rather than a dialect, without, however, having an army and a navy. In other words, all dialects are languages (in the sense of perfectly formed human idioms), but not all languages are dialects, because an idiom is considered a dialect insofar as it represents a 'lower' level subordinated to a 'higher' one.

The term 'dialect' derives from the Greek *diálektos*, which means 'speech' or the language of a country or region, with reference in particular to the Greek literary languages, Ionic, Attic, and so on. In the Roman tradition, which put a higher price on uniformity, the Latin adaptation *dialectus* was hardly used at all. The notion reappears in the Renaissance, with the Italian humanists. The first attestation in Latin seems to be in Valla, before 1444, and then in Filelfo (1473), Poliziano (1486–7), and others. In Italian the first known attestation seems to be in Niccolò Liburnio (1546) and then in Varchi (1570 [finished 1564]), Salviati (1584), etc.[4] The notion was designated by other terms, however, in preference to *dialectus*, *dialetto*. Among the words used, we find in Latin *idioma* and *proprietas* (or the more general *lingua*, *sermo*, *loquela*) and their Italian counterparts *idioma* and *proprietà*. Conceptually, in the late

Quattrocento, the mediation of Greek was crucial for the passage from the fixity of Latin to the more varied multiplicity of the vernacular, as Dionisotti pointed out.[5] It is through the Italian humanists that the word and the notion of dialect spread to French, English, and German from the middle of the sixteenth century.

The second and third questions are: Which are the Italian dialects? Where do they come from? In the context of English, 'dialect' is often used to refer to varieties of English. In the Italian context 'dialect' does not refer to varieties of Italian. Like Italian (or rather, Tuscan, on which Italian is based), Italian dialects are different Romance languages deriving from Latin. Neapolitan, Milanese, Venetian, and so on are sisters of Tuscan, not varieties of it. From this angle one could say that Tuscan itself is one of the Italian dialects, or else, which amounts to the same thing, that the Italian dialects are not dialects but languages. Returning to the considerations about the sociolinguistic distinction between higher (or superordinate) and lower (or subordinate) levels, one could say that the term 'dialect' is inappropriate to the linguistic situation of Italy in the thirteenth century. There was Latin, and there were different vernaculars. Some of the vernaculars, such as that of the Sicilian School, aimed at achieving a higher, more standardized, supra-regional literary form. Tuscan, or more precisely literary Florentine, represented by the works of Dante, Petrarch, and Boccaccio, was particularly successful in realizing this aim during the fourteenth century. This was publicly consecrated through the codification offered by Bembo's *Prose* (1525).

Which, then, are the Italian dialects? One not unreasonable answer could be similar to that given by Dante at the beginning of the Trecento, when he lists fourteen subdivisions. Modern classifications also tend to have groups coinciding with regions: Ligurian, Piedmontese, Venetan, Emilian, Tuscan, Umbrian and Laziale,

Marchigiano, Abruzzese, Campano, Lucano, Pugliese, Calabrese, Sicilian, Sardinian. If the classification needs to be more precise, taking into account finer distinctions, then the number of different dialects could easily reach hundreds, or even thousands of varieties, one for each village, or even for each district of a town. Here, too, one could recall Dante, who observed (*De vulgari eloquentia*, I, IX, 4) that in Bologna people who live in the Strada Maggiore speak differently from those of Borgo San Felice in the outskirts.

If I may open a parenthesis, I should say that this conclusion is unwelcome, but there is no way of estimating 'scientifically' the degree of difference that justifies calling two varieties 'different languages.' The standard lists of the languages of the world give figures from about 3,000 (Décsy)[6] to about 6,000 (Grimes).[7] Gyula Décsy mentions that Italian is spoken with many distinct regional variations, which is at best too vague and at worst misleading. Barbara Grimes's list of thirty-three languages in Italy, which does not inspire full confidence, relies on rather doubtful authorities and, particularly concerning the so-called Italian dialects, looks positively bizarre.

One of the questions we asked above is: Where do the Italian dialects come from? The answer is: They derive from spoken Latin; that is, they replaced Latin, or rather, they are what Latin became, from around the middle of the first millennium A.D. Why did Latin not develop into one single vernacular in Italy but change instead into the many different idioms I have mentioned? The assumption that has prevailed since the nineteenth century, with Ascoli and the founding of Italian dialectology, is that the difference between dialects is due more to factors of 'substratum' than to those of 'superstratum,' that is, to the different ways in which Latin was learnt by the populations that inhabited Italy before the Roman conquest: the Celts, Veneti, Etruscans, Umbrians, Oscans, and so on, who imposed onto Latin certain features (particularly phonological ones) of their original languages. This is thought to have been more important for the formation of the Italian dialects than the influence of the languages of conquering populations, such as the Goths, Lombards, and Franks; these 'superstratum' features are thought to concern lexical borrowing and place names, rather than phonology.

When Latin stopped being spoken and when it was replaced by the vernacular are controversial issues. The first dated vernacular document is the *Placito capuano* (Sao ko kelle terre) of 960. The earliest text, if it can be called vernacular rather than Latin, is the so-called *Indovinello veronese* (*Se pareba boues*), of uncertain date and origin – possibly of the early ninth century from Verona, or possibly earlier, from Pisa or even Sardinia or Spain.

Dating the origin of the vernacular in speech is even more problematic. Many philologists propose a time round the sixth century, but considering individual phenomena and interpreting them in terms of substratum, one can go much further back and identify, for instance, the origins of the southern Italian [nn]<[nd] (as in *quanno* from Latin *quando* 'when') as an Oscan development. Suggesting, however, that in Pompei they spoke Neapolitan in the first century A.D. would be going too far.

What are Italian dialects like? For those who may have met examples of standard Italian but not of dialects, I think that a few comparisons may suffice to show that they are actually different languages. The word for 'Sunday' in Italian is *domenica* (the Tuscan *domenica*), from the Latin *dominica* (*dies*) 'the day of the Lord' (*dominus*). From the same Latin form arise the Venetian *domenega*, the Bolognese *dmandga*, the Neapolitan *rummeneca*, the Palermitan *duminica*. These are straightforward developments, according to the respective phonological laws of the individual dialects, from the same Latin word. Dialects, of course, can use words that have different etymologies. To quote Venetian, a dialect that is familiar to me, the word for 'fork,' Italian (Tuscan) *forchetta*,

Greek *piruni*); the word for 'chair,' Italian (Tuscan) *sedia* or *seggiola*, from the root of the Latin *sedere*, is *carega*, from the Greek *kathédra*, through the Latin *cathedra* (this is also the etymology of the French *chaire*, *chaise*, English *chair*).

So much for the dialects, at least for the moment. The final topic I want to mention in the first section of this chapter are the minority languages. Traditionally, discussion of the Italian dialects is kept separate from that of the so-called foreign-speaking minorities ('minoranze alloglotte'). Rather than 'minority languages,' some prefer to call them 'less used languages' in an attempt, not obviously successful or even well founded, to avoid giving offence. These are communities (generally established in Italy for many centuries) using idioms historically distinct from those used by the larger population into which the minority is inserted. From the current literature we can retrieve the following list (with figures, often hypothetical and approximate, for the number of speakers):

(a) Small 'historical' relics, mostly from the fifteenth and sixteenth centuries: Greek (30,000) and Albanian (100,000) in southern Italy; Catalan (15,000) at Alghero in Sardinia; German (13,000) in small communities in Piedmont and in the Veneto; Croat (3,000) in the Molise; Occitanic and Franco-Provençal in small colonies in southern Italy: according to Tagliavini[8] in northeastern Sicily, provinces of Messina and Enna (Sanfratello, Piazza Armerina, Nicosia, Sperlinga, Novara, Aidone) and in Basilicata and near the gulf of Policastro. There are also Genoese colonies (Carloforte and Calasetta in Sardinia; Bonifacio in Corsica), and Emilian colonies (Gombitello, near Camaiore in Versilia; Sillano in the Serchio valley).

(b) Stronger groups, established in the vicinity of larger communities using that idiom in a foreign country: German (280,000) in the Alto Adige (South Tyrol); Occitanic and Franco-Provençal (115,000) in Piedmont; Slovene (53,000) in the Veneto.

(c) In the classification of Romance languages, Friulian (625,000) and Dolomitic Ladin (50,000) (both usually grouped under the label 'Rhaeto-Romance,' with the Romansh dialects of the Grisons in Switzerland) and Sardinian (estimated between 160,000 and 1,200,000) are sometimes associated with the Italian dialects, and sometimes separated from them as independent Romance varieties.

(d) Some lists also give Romani (Gypsy) (16,000), Judaeo-Italian (of debated nature and extension), the Italian Sign Language, and finally the languages of the recent immigrants from central and northern Africa (figures estimated at over 1 million), of whom it is not clear how many will become permanent residents of Italy and whether they will preserve their original languages.

## 2. *The Use of Italian and Dialects*

The first point I examined in this chapter concerns the standard, the dialects, and the so-called minority languages. I should now like to look briefly at the second point, which concerns the use of dialect and Italian relative to each other. The data are those provided by the ISTAT (Istituto per le ricerche statistiche) on the basis of questionnaires distributed on six occasions between 1964 and 1996. One must consider the relative smallness of the sample used: 1,985 people in 1996 (but the margin of error for percentages referred to the whole population is ±2 per cent); and also the fact that the questionnaires ask for self-evaluation, and there is no external checking of linguistic behaviour.

One can observe variations according to age, sex, level of education, region and size of the relevant conurbation. The figures concerning the use of Italian are higher for younger people, for women, for people with a higher level of education, for central Italy and the northwest, and for larger conurbations. The reasons for these differences are fairly obvious, apart from those concerning gender: on the basis of traditional assumptions about different patterns of behaviour according to gender, one might have expected women (compared with men) either to use the dialect more, because they spend more time at home and have fewer occasions to be engaged in public or professional activities requiring Italian; or, conversely, to use the dialect less, because they are more sensitive to the requirements of fashion and social advancement implying the use of Italian and less subject to the pressures of working-class solidarity, which encourages the use of the dialect. Both assumptions, however, are likely not to correspond to contemporary cultural and social conditions, and the interpretation of gender differences, with women using the dialect slightly less than men both at home and outside, 'does not seem easy to explain,' as the authors of the report observe.[9] In fact, one might expect the opposite, considering that both older persons and the less educated are more numerous in the sample of women than in that of men. The difference concerning the use of Italian in the home, with women using more Italian than men, may be related to the fact that women speak more frequently with children – a context in which dialect is often avoided. The data are as follows:

|                            | 1974 | 1982 | 1988 | 1991 | 1996 |
|----------------------------|------|------|------|------|------|
| *At home*                  | %    | %    | %    | %    | %    |
| Dialect with everyone      | 51   | 47   | 40   | 36   | 34   |
| Italian with everyone      | 25   | 29   | 34   | 34   | 34   |
| *With friends and colleagues* |      |      |      |      |      |
| Only or mainly dialect     | 42   | 36   | 33   | 23   | 28   |
| Only or mainly Italian     | 36   | 42   | 47   | 48   | 50   |

Each one of us who has been in contact with the Italian linguistic situation is likely to have some personal, anecdotal evidence concerning either the use of Italian in unexpected circumstances or the exceptional vigour of the dialect, which refuses to die in the midst of the most radically modern technological, social, and economic developments. The data provided by the Doxa Bulletins could be used to support either impression. When we look at them dispassionately, however, they seem to suggest at least the following considerations:

(a) There is an overall decline in the use of the dialect, accompanied by a parallel increase in the use of Italian, both in the home and outside. What is striking is the slowness of this process and the extraordinary tenacity of the dialects.

(b) In the period between the last two inquiries, 1991 and 1996, certain aspects of this process seem to have stopped, or even to reveal a change of direction. The use of Italian with all relatives, in the home, has remained stable at 34 per cent (in fact, this figure has not changed since 1988), and the use mainly or exclusively of the dialect with friends and colleagues, outside the home, has increased from 23 to 28 per cent.

(c) Before we make generalizations about the direction in which language use is moving, it would be useful to keep in mind the following: in 1996, 136 years after the proclamation of the Italian state, the figure for the use mainly or exclusively of Italian with friends and colleagues outside the home has grown, for the first time in Italian history, reaching 50 per cent of the population. On the other hand, the use in the home, with all relatives, seems as good an indication as any of which idiom can be considered the mother tongue, that is, of which idiom people are native speakers. In 1996 the figure is the same (34 per cent) for Italian and for the dialect.

In conclusion, we can note that the main difference between today and the years of unification seems to be that then Italy was effectively a monolingual country, with the local dialect being the only idiom known to the vast majority of the population, while now it is largely a bilingual country.

### 3. *Language Policy*

The final part of this chapter concerns language policy. We can distinguish three different periods after unification. Between 1861 and 1918 monoglot assumptions prevail. The Piedmontese law which authorized the use of French in the Valle d'Aosta was abrogated. Dialects were generally ignored (notwithstanding some proposals from the more enlightened educationalists to use them as starting points for the learning of Italian). The ministry of education encouraged the use of school grammars inspired by the Manzonian project of favouring Florentine usage, even where it differed from standard Italian (*core* for *cuore*, *verrai anche te* for *verrai anche tu*, *anderò* for *andrò*, *la era sana* for *era sana*, etc.); for a general discussion see the volume by Maria Catricalà.[10]

In the period between 1918 and 1945 we find an attempt to impose linguistic assimilation, including forced Italianization of surnames and place names and the imposition of Italian as the medium for education, even in those communities in northern and eastern Veneto where schoolchildren were monolingual speakers of German or Slovenian.

After 1945 the Constitution of the Republic adopted a pluralist line. Article 6 of the Constitution affirms: 'The Republic safeguards linguistic minorities with appropriate laws' (La Repubblica tutela con apposite norme le minoranze linguistiche). Little has been done, however, to enact or even to interpret this article and to clarify its terms of reference.

Action was taken to protect two 'strong' minorities whose language is linked to that of an adjacent foreign state.[11] For the Valle d'Aosta a 'bilingual' assumption was adopted, under which all citizens should be able to understand both the minority (French) and the majority (Italian) language. For German in Alto Adige and Slovenian in Friuli-Venezia Giulia a 'separatist' or 'apartheid' model was adopted, according to which the members of one community are not expected to know the language of the other community. Public servants must be able to use both languages, and schooling is separate, individual schools using one language as the medium of instruction while the other is studied as a foreign language. This arrangement guarantees the protection of the minority language (which may be, of course, the language of the majority in the relevant region) but does not encourage the learning of the national language. For instance, even now, Italian seems to be little known by the German-speaking majority in the province of Bolzano.

A bill for the protection of linguistic minorities (Proposta di legge N. 612: *Norme in materia di tutela delle minoranze linguistiche*) was passed by the Chamber of Deputies on 20 November 1991, but it could not be voted on by the Senate, since the government fell (for reasons unconnected with the minority languages) and Parliament was dissolved. This bill precipitated a series of polemical discussions in the daily press, as well as contributions by linguists.[12] It was resubmitted to the Chamber in 1996, discussed and approved by Chamber and Senate in 1997–9, and finally passed, as Law N. 482, on 15 December 1999 (*Gazzetta Ufficiale della Repubblica Italiana*, N. 297, 20 December 1999). The law is called 'Norme in materia di tutela delle minoranze linguistiche storiche.' The addition of the term 'historical' (storiche) was apparently intended to explain the omission from the list of linguistic minorities of the idioms of recent immigrants from China, north and central Africa, etc., whose linguistic and educational needs are being dealt with separately. The list of languages and cultures to be protected (Art. 2) mentions the 'Albanian, Catalan, German, Greek, Slovene, Croatian populations, and those speaking French, Franco-Provençal, Friulian, Ladin, Occitan, and Sardinian' (popolazioni albanesi, catalane, germaniche, greche, slovene e croate, e ... quelle parlanti il francese, il franco-provenzale, il friulano, il ladino, l'occitano e il sardo). The law provides a moderate degree of recognition to the relevant minority languages, allowing their use (if a stated percentage of those involved require it) as the medium in kindergartens and elementary and lower secondary schools, in the proceedings of borough councils, in certain courts of law, in state radio and television broadcasts, and so forth.

The mention of Friulian and Sardinian in the original 1991 version, had made the bill appear, to some of its critics, as a Pandora's box – or perhaps a can of worms. If the law was meant to apply to Friulian and Sardinian (and now also to Ladin), why not, for example, to Piedmontese, Lombard, Veneto, as well? This seemed to encourage the most extreme demands of the 'Leghe' political groups, which wanted the dialects to be accepted as official languages of the regions, and finally to start the undoing of the Risorgimento and the breaking up of the Italian state.

Undoubtedly the designation 'minoranze linguistiche storiche,' even if it was introduced for different reasons, as we saw above, in the Italian context appears to refer to the Albanian, Greek, and other minorities, not to the Italian dialects (Piedmontese, Lombard, etc.), and, as a matter of fact, the passing of the law in 1999 did not evoke the excited polemics caused by the 1991 bill. On the other hand, it is also true that in the Italian cultural tradition the status of Friulian, Ladin, and Sardinian has always been a moot point, some dialectologists including them in the panorama of the Italian dialects (in a way in which Albanian, Greek, etc. are not) and others considering them to be separate Romance varieties.

Another objection made against the 1991 bill was that most of the idioms it is meant to protect are effectively no longer alive: they are reduced to the state of 'historical' relics, to a large degree assimilated into Italian and/or the encircling dialects, surviving, if at all, in a state of fragmentation and without an accepted standard variety. The practical consequences of this law remain to be seen. If, as well as helping people whose rights need protection, it will also encourage better information concerning these linguistic minorities, it will be all to the good. It is difficult to say how it will affect the conditions of Sardinian, Friulian, and Ladin and whether it will also have indirect consequences for the traditional Italian dialects.[13] If I were to rewrite this chapter in a few years' time, I suspect I would need to modify not only this third section but the first and second as well.

NOTES

1 Tullio De Mauro, *Storia linguistica dell'Italia unita* (Bari: Laterza, 1963).

2 Arrigo Castellani, 'Quanti erano gl'italofoni nel 1861?' *Studi linguistici italiani* 8 (1982), 3–26.

3 Giulio Lepschy, 'Dialect and Language: A Brief Introduction,' in *Italian Dialects and Literature: From the Renaissance to the Present*, ed. Emmanuela Tandello and Diego Zancani (London: Institute of Romance Studies, 1996), Supplement 1, *Journal of the Institute of Romance Studies*, 1–6; in Italian in Anna Laura Lepschy and Giulio Lepschy, *L'amanuense analfabeta e altri saggi* (Florence: Olschki, 1999), 145–52.

4 See Mario Alinei, '"Dialetto": Un concetto rinascimentale fiorentino,' *Quaderni di semantica* 2 (1981), 147–73 (also in Mario Alinei, *Lingua e dialetti: struttura, storia e geografia* [Bologna: il Mulino, 1984], 69–99) and Paolo Trovato, '"Dialetto" e sinonimi ("idioma," "proprietà," "lingua") nella terminologia linguistica quattro- e cinquecentesca,' *Rivista di letteratura italiana* 2 (1984), 205–36.

5 Carlo Dionisotti, *Gli umanisti e il volgare fra Quattro e Cinquecento* (Florence: Le Monnier, 1968).

6 Gyula Décsy, *Statistical Report on the Languages of the World as of 1985* (Bloomington, Ind.: Eurolingua, 1986–8).

7  Barbara Grimes, *Ethnologue: Languages of the World* (Dallas, Tex.: Summer Institute of Linguistics, 1996; 1st ed., 1951).

8  Carlo Tagliavini, *Le origini delle lingue neolatine: Introduzione alla filologia romanza*, 6th ed. (Bologna: Pàtron, 1972), 400.

9  DOXA, 'L'uso del dialetto,' *Bollettino* 50, nn.16, 17 (1996), 167–85, 170.

10  Maria Catricalà, *Le grammatiche scolastiche dell'italiano edite dal 1860 al 1918* (Florence: Accademia della Crusca, 1991).

11  Arnaldo Pizzorusso, 'Minoranze etnico-linguistiche,' in *Enciclopedia del diritto*, vol. 26 (Milan: Giuffrè, 1976), 527–58; Massimo Stipo, 'Minoranze etnico-linguistiche: Il Diritto pubblico,' in *Enciclopedia giuridica* (Rome: Istituto della Enciclopedia italiana, 1992), 1–12.

12  Reservations against the bill in Tristano Bolelli, 'Le minoranze linguistiche in Italia,' *Atti della Accademia dei Lincei: Classe di scienze morali, storiche e filologiche: Rendiconti* 9:3 (1992), 1–8; Raffaele Simone, 'Minoranze in minoranza,' *Italiano & oltre* 7:1 (1992) 3–4. A defence of the bill appears in Tullio De Mauro, 'Una legge per le lingue,' *Rivista dei libri* (Sept. 1992), 12–14; (Oct. 1992), 11–13. Tullio De Mauro has been mentioned as one of the experts who inspired this bill.

13  As this volume is being prepared, I read that Alleanza Nazionale (a so-called post-fascist party) has presented to the Chamber of Deputies a bill asking for the insertion into the Constitution of the statement, 'The Italian language is the official language of the Republic' (La lingua italiana è la lingua ufficiale della Repubblica) (*Corriere della Sera*, 7 August 2001). One wonders whether this is meant to encourage citizens to learn Italian better, or to dissuade them from using other languages.

# CHAPTER THREE

# *Popular Italian: Fact or Fiction?*

The title of this chapter consists of two parts. The first part presents a topic (Popular Italian),[1] and the second, in the form of a question, suggests that we should try to decide whether in looking at this topic we are examining questions of fact or dealing with subjective problems of our own creation rather than with objective features belonging to an external reality. The question is only apparently straightforward, even if we leave out the distinction of a more general nature, which seems to dominate contemporary theory, between I and E, that is, Internal and External linguistics. However, although a straight answer is not forthcoming, I hope that by the end our ideas will be clearer than at the start.

In this chapter I propose, first, to look at the way in which the expression 'popular Italian' (and similar designations in other European traditions) has been used; second, to consider the emergence of the notion of 'popular Italian,' particularly in the 1970s, as a topic crucial to an understanding of the way in which Italian is used in Italy; third, to analyse some examples, in the areas of phonology, spelling, morphology, vocabulary and syntax, which I hope will illustrate and clarify the notion of popular Italian; and fourth, to draw some provisional conclusions.

## 1. *'Popular Italian'*
The term 'popular Italian' is generally assumed to have been modelled on the French designation *français populaire.'* The French is

less uncertain and controversial than the Italian. It is used as the title of a 1920 volume by Henri Bauche,[2] and seems to canonize the topic as a legitimate subject of general interest by appearing in the well-known series *'Que sais-je?': Le français populaire*, by Pierre Guiraud.[3] *Français populaire* has its own grammatical and lexical features, which distinguish it from *le bon usage*, to use the title of the standard grammar by Maurice Grevisse.[4] In German we find the expression, *Unsere Umgang[s]sprache*, in the title of the monograph by Hermann Wunderlich,[5] contrasted to *Hochsprache*. In fact, *Umgangssprache* can also designate the ordinary language of everyday communication.[6] There is an interesting study by Leo Spitzer called *Italienische Umgangssprache*, which covers features of ordinary Italian but not popular Italian.[7] The latter is actually discussed by Spitzer[8] in his analysis of the letters of Italian prisoners of war in Austria during the First World War, which is one of the first detailed studies of popular Italian.[8]

For English we find expressions such as 'dialect' (not in the more technical sense of a variety of English geographically or historically distinct from the standard, but in the sense of substandard, i.e., a usage deemed to be 'socially' inferior), and designations such as 'vernacular' and 'demotic' contrasted with the standard and (perhaps especially in Britain) 'the Queen's (or King's) English.' I have sometimes been asked by Italian colleagues why there seem to be no studies of popular English, when there are so many discussions of popular Italian. The answer is, I suppose, partly cultural and historical and partly terminological. In the history of English culture, the distance between the literary and the colloquial language is narrower than it is for Italian: there is a sense in which English, without specification, can be deemed to be 'popular' in a way in which Italian cannot. On the other hand, from a terminological viewpoint, one could argue that most sociolinguistic studies of English deal with some sort of 'popular' language rather than with the standard, literary variety analysed and codified by traditional grammatical descriptions. Certain features are obvious and immediately recognizable, such as *we was* for the standard *we were*, or *them* for *those* (as in *open them windows*), or the multiple negative constructions (as in *I don't want nothing*).

Other cases are less easily placed. An interesting article by Peter Trudgill concerning the difficulties in judging varieties that differ from one's own was prepared at the University of Reading.[9] Trudgill asked different groups of informants, including (i) foreign students, and (ii) lecturers in linguistics who were native speakers of English, to classify certain sentences according to a scale that included judgments such as, 'I do not use it, but I have heard it used'; 'I have not heard it used, but I imagine someone might use it'; also, 'only a foreigner could use it,' and 'no human being is likely to use it.'

The results were somewhat unexpected. For instance, when assessing the sentence (a) *Look – is that a man stands there?* about 45 per cent of linguistics lecturers considered it likely to be used only by a foreigner, and another 45 per cent as unlikely to be used by anyone. Among the foreign students, the result was 47 per cent in both cases. The sentence is, in fact, common in the East Anglian variety of which Trudgill is an expert. Even more surprising were the judgments about (b) *My hair needs washed*, which is used by over 4 million native speakers in Scotland, in English districts adjacent to the Scottish border, and in parts of the United States. Forty-five per cent of the linguistics lecturers and 28 per cent of the foreign students thought that only a foreigner would use the sentence, and 27 per cent of the lecturers and 61 per cent of the foreign students thought that it was unlikely that anyone would use it: unsuitable for human consumption. Disagreements, even though to a lesser degree, may, of course, occur in judging sentences not only from a 'popular' variety, but also from the standard language, both for English and for Italian.

## 2. *The Origin of the Designation*

The second point I propose to examine is the spread of the expression 'italiano popolare' in discussions about the Italian language in the 1970s. The notion of popular Italian needs to be contrasted with the notions of regional Italian and spoken Italian.[10] These three notions were at the centre of the attention of Italian linguists in three successive decades, that of regional Italian in the 1960s, that of popular Italian in the 1970s, and that of spoken Italian in the 1980s.[11] In the 1990s there seems to have been a reduction of the more notable peculiarities in all three areas, accompanied by a gradual acceptance of some of their features as part of the norm.[12] Consequently, the written standard appears now, at the opening of the new century, to encompass certain characteristics that traditionally were thought to be typically regional, or popular, or spoken. By the same token, this change makes it more difficult both to trace a precise outline of these three areas and to attribute to each of them any specific individual expression.

There are two main studies of popular Italian, both dating from about thirty years ago, one by Tullio De Mauro and one by Manlio Cortelazzo.[13] De Mauro, one of the main Italian linguists, was for a time, before the second Berlusconi government, minister of education in Italy. He is an expert on semantics, editor of the largest dictionary of modern Italian usage,[14] and author of the standard history of modern Italian, the *Storia linguistica dell'Italia unita*. As early as 1963, in the first edition of this work,[15] De Mauro mentioned 'unitary popular Italian' (Italiano popolare unitario), a phenomenon that became substantial during the First World War, when millions of Italian soldiers, mostly dialect speakers, were thrown together in the war zone of the Veneto region. In these circumstances they elaborated a common idiom that revealed most of the features subsequently to reappear when masses from different regions strove to use the national language in the course of their struggle for social and economic improvement. This ambition accompanied their attempt to escape from the dialect 'ghettoes' in which illiterates were confined. It was a rough, uncouth, unsophisticated idiom, but it was lively, vigorous, and spontaneous, more flexible and vivacious than the turgid, pedantic, artificially literary sort of Italian that schools used to impose on dialect speakers. It was 'unitary,' De Mauro suggested, not because it had no regional features (these were, of course, present and immediately perceivable, particularly in pronunciation), but in its aim, which was to use the national language instead of the regional dialect. It was also in a sense 'progressive,' since it contained the seeds of an idiom that was to become an authentically popular language, spoken and written, common to the whole nation.

Manlio Cortelazzo is one of the main Italian dialectologists and a specialist of Venetan (if I may use a recent neologism to denote the dialects of the Veneto region, reserving Venetian for one of the Veneto dialects, i.e., that of Venice). In a volume of 1972 Cortelazzo presents a detailed analysis of popular Italian. He has a sympathetic, if slightly patronizing, attitude towards the users of popular Italian, whose education has been insufficient. The starting point is, of course, the peculiar historical condition of Italy in which, traditionally, individuals are native speakers of their local dialects (including the Tuscan ones) and the national language is a literary idiom, mainly used in writing, which is learnt through education. The definition of popular Italian offered by Cortelazzo is as follows: 'the kind of Italian which has been imperfectly acquired by those who have a dialect as their mother tongue' (il tipo di italiano imperfettamente acquisito da chi ha per madrelingua il dialetto). As can be seen, the definition is backward looking, rather than forward looking like that of De Mauro. In fact, the assumptions on which the definition is based changed during the second half of the twentieth century. It is possible to argue that for people born after

1950, having grown up in the age of television, Italian has become, for the first time in the country's history, a native language with native speakers, in a sense comparable to that which applies to other languages, such as English and French. As a result, the basis on which popular Italian can be defined has changed.

Both De Mauro and Cortelazzo base their comments about popular Italian mainly on written texts, such as letters or diaries produced by people who were semi-literate.[16] It is not always clear, however, which of two different assumptions lies at the basis of these studies (or even whether the necessary distinctions have been made). One assumption is that popular Italian is typically spoken – it is the way in which Italian is spoken – by people who are unfamiliar with the literary language; and the texts that are analysed simply reflect the speech of these people, whereas normally a written text is composed according to rules and conventions that are those of educated speakers. The other assumption is that popular Italian is essentially a written phenomenon: a text in popular Italian represents what is produced in writing by people who are unfamiliar with the conventions of the literary tradition, that is, with the code that rules written expressions at all levels, from spelling, to lexical choice, to morphosyntax. A spoken expression can be as informal, vernacular, demotic, substandard as one likes. It becomes popular only when it is written, that is, when it reveals that the user is unable to control the rules governing written communication. If we look at individual examples from written texts, in a majority of cases it is fairly easy to decide whether or not it is a question of popular Italian. In the case of examples from speech it is more difficult to decide whether what we hear is an informal, colloquial, regional expression, or whether it can be appropriately classified as belonging to popular Italian.

A further difficulty, which perhaps can be related to the Chomskian distinction between I and E language and the available literature does not clarify sufficiently, is caused by not deciding whether popular Italian is appropriate for defining individual expressions or the language of individual speakers. If we consider a sentence such as *a me questo non mi piace* ('I don't like this,' literally, 'to me this is not pleasing to me,' with both pronouns in the dative, the first stressed and the second unstressed), we may find that the question 'Is this an example of popular Italian?' is not easy to answer. In the first place we may have to decide whether it is an instance of colloquial, informal, spoken Italian, perhaps illustrating that well-known syntactic phenomenon called 'left dislocation,' which consists in moving a stressed complement (*a me*) to the front of the sentence, and replacing it, in the appropriate position, with a clitic (*mi*). In this case it need have nothing to do with popular Italian. Second, we have to go beyond the individual sentence, and establish the degree of competence of the speakers. It seems obvious that if the speakers are choosing, for whatever reason, *a me questo non mi piace* over other forms available to them (such as, *a me questo non piace* and *questo non mi piace*), it would be misleading to say that they are using popular Italian. This judgment might instead be appropriate for speakers whose knowledge of standard Italian is insufficient to allow them a choice between these three possibilities and who can use only the structure, modelled on dialect, in which the two pronouns (*a me* and *mi*) coexist.

## 3. *Some Examples*

In the third part of this chapter, I should like to mention some examples of popular Italian with the aim, on the one hand, of briefly illustrating the phenomenon we are discussing and, on the other, of showing that the classification of individual data is usually controversial, ambiguous, or open to different interpretations.

The examples, in fact, could easily be multiplied or replaced by others. I shall choose them from different areas: (a) phonology, (b) spelling, (c) morphology, (d) vocabulary, (e) syntax.[17]

### 3.1. *Phonology*

As is well known (for reasons that are fairly well understood connected with the spread of standard Italian as a written rather than a spoken language), pronunciation has remained an area in which regional variations are found and, in my opinion, are largely accepted. How largely, however, is still controversial. Tuscan (more specifically educated Florentine) is generally assumed to represent the norm, but there are certain phonological features, both in the north and in the south, that differ from the Tuscan ones and are almost universally used in their respective regions. Particularly in the north some of these features (but not others) are generally accepted as standard, even though they differ from Tuscan usage.

For instance, in the north, word-initial affricates (as in ['dzi:o] *zio* 'uncle') and intervocalic sibilants (as in ['ka:za] *casa* 'house') are systematically voiced. In Tuscan these words have a voiceless consonant (['tsi:o], ['ka:sa]), and the opposition between voiceless and voiced is distinctive: *zannata* [tsan'na:ta] 'a tearing with fangs' vs [dzan'na:ta] 'a comic scene, as if of a Zanni,' and internally *razza* ['rattsa] 'race, sort' vs ['raddza] 'skate' (the fish); and *fuso* ['fu:so] 'spindle' vs ['fu:zo] 'fused,' *chiese* ['kjɛ:se] 'asked' vs ['kjɛ:ze] 'churches.'

Syntactic doubling (a complex system of rules that establish the conditions of consonant strengthening in word-initial position) is unknown in the north: *a casa* 'home' (= 'to the house'), northern [a 'ka:za] vs Tuscan [a k'ka:sa].

Intervocalic affricates are always strengthened in Tuscan irrespective of the spelling: in the north the pronunciation usually corresponds to the spelling, but one can also hear 'substandard,' dialectal pronunciations, which replace the affricate with a sibilant: *stazione* 'station,' northern [sta'tsjo:ne], dialectal (Venetan) [sta'sjo:ne], vs Tuscan [stat'tsjo:ne].

Voiced intervocalic bilabial stops and voiced intervocalic prepalatal affricates are always strengthened in central and southern Italian. In Tuscan the intervocalic prepalatal affricate is usually replaced by a fricative: *abito* 'I reside,' southern ['abbito], vs Tuscan ['a:bito]; *magico* 'magical,' southern ['maddʒiko], vs northern ['ma:dʒiko], Tuscan ['ma:ʒiko].

According to purists, all the pronunciations that differ from the Tuscan version are, in a sense, wrong, based on an insufficient knowledge of the standard, and it seems that, strictly speaking, they ought to be considered instances of popular Italian. Common sense usually prevails, however, and more realistic judgments are made. I think that many (if not most) educated Italians would find it bizarre and unbelievable for ['dzi:o], ['ka:za], [a 'ka:za], [sta'tsjo:ne] to be described as instances of popular Italian. On the other hand, [sta'sjo:ne] would be considered dialectal and substandard (popular Italian) even in the Veneto region (although it may be used in ordinary conversation even by people who have a good command of the standard written language and who could not be appropriately described as users of popular Italian).

Similar, but not identical, is the case of ['abbito] and ['maddʒiko] which can be (and, in fact, usually are) used in the south not only by the uneducated but also by people who have a perfect grasp of the literary language. From this point of view, although they are felt to be non-standard in Tuscany and in the north, their use cannot be defined as belonging to popular Italian.

More problematic is the Tuscan pronunciation ['ma:ʒiko], which is not used either in the north or in the centre-south and is not recommended in the current descriptions of the standard. It is normal, however, for Tuscan speakers, including the most highly educated, and for this reason it cannot be described as belonging to popular Italian according to the definition cited.

### 3.2. *Spelling*

Spelling conventions in Italian are standardized to a considerable degree, and, in fact, deviations (spelling mistakes, 'errori d'ortografia') are a typical indicator of insufficient competence in the literary language. Here, too, before considering an individual deviation as typical of popular Italian, one needs to establish what a person knows about its usage.

According to a commonly taught rule, for words in *–cia* the plural is in *–cie* if the *-c-* is preceded by a vowel (*camicia* 'shirt,' plural *camicie*), and in *–ce* if it is preceded by a consonant (*lancia* 'spear,' plural *lance*). Therefore *provincia* ought to have the plural *province*. If one finds the plural *provincie*, this could be a misspelling (and be interpreted as one of the signs of orthographic uncertainty characteristic of popular Italian), or it could be a more learned spelling, which preserves the *-i-* of the Latin plural *provinciae*.

Similarly, *familiare* ('familiar' and 'of the family') is the traditional spelling, and *famigliare* could be a (popular Italian) mistake, or a more sophisticated spelling aiming at distinguishing *familiare* 'familiar' from *famigliare* 'of the family,' or a deliberate preference for a vernacular rather than a Latinizing spelling.

The grammar-book rule suggests *qual è* (which is) without apostrophe, similar to *qual amico, qual amica* (which friend) both cases of truncation (as in *qual donna* 'which woman'), unlike the pair *un amico, un'amica* (a friend), in which the first is a case of truncation (*un amico*, like *un dono* 'a gift') and the second a case of elision (*un'amica*, unlike *una donna* 'a woman'). This convention is now codified, but has little historical justification, and some highly learned authors (Riccardo Bacchelli, for instance) prefer to write *qual'è* with an apostrophe. Faced by the spelling *qual'è*, we have to decide whether it is an orthographic mistake, due to ignorance of the rule, or whether it is a sophisticated choice that deliberately follows literary models and overrules recent grammar-book conventions.

### 3.3. *Morphology*

Morphology is also highly standardized in Italian. Certain forms, such as *venghino* for *vengano*, are almost a stereotype of popular Italian, as in *venghino, signori, venghino*, which can be rendered as 'come, all ye good people.' Exactly for this reason, faced by a *venghino*, one has to decide whether the speaker thinks that is the correct form, or whether a deliberate allusion to popular Italian usage is intended.

In other cases it is a question of regional variation. In the literary language *arancia* (feminine) means the fruit 'orange,' and *arancio* (masculine) 'orange tree.' In the Veneto region the ordinary word for 'orange' is *arancio* (although in the Venetian dialect the form is feminine: *naransa*). Since it is used also by people who have a highly sophisticated control of the literary language, it is legitimate to hesitate before calling it a case of popular Italian.

Similarly, the gerund of *disfare* (to undo) is *disfacendo* in the literary language, and *disfando* more colloquially (see *io disfo* vs *io disfaccio*). Again, one may wonder how appropriate it is to refer to popular Italian in such cases.

### 3.4. *Vocabulary*

The difference between regional forms is so strong in Italian that in many cases the dialectal term may be more widely used locally than the standard one, which has not been able to shake off a parochial, Tuscan colouring and to acquire a national currency, notwithstanding the support it receives from current dictionaries. As is to be expected, the weaker an allegedly standard expression is in a national perspective, the more problematic it is to qualify as popular Italian the regional equivalent, which tends to be considered more expressive or appropriate and can be described as 'popular' in the sense of 'widely used,' rather than in the sense specified above of revealing an 'imperfectly acquired' knowledge of Italian. A few examples, with reference to regional Veneto usage, will suffice.

The word for trousers in Italian is *pantaloni* or *calzoni*. The coexistence of two terms, as often happens in Italian, is indicative of a weakness, rather than a strength of the usage, in that there is uncertainty about possible differences of meaning or nuance. We want to keep synchrony and diachrony distinct, of course, but this does not imply that usage disregards the historical connotations and richness of a term. From this viewpoint it is instructive to consult good historical and etymological dictionaries, such as those by Battaglia and Cortelazzo-Zolli.

The word *pantaloni* comes from the garment of the Commedia dell'Arte figure of Pantalone (Pantaleone);[18] in Baretti we find *pantalonata*, and in Gozzi *pantalonicamente*. In Genovesi (1791) *Pantalonessa* means a 'woman who puts on an authoritarian attitude' (donna che assume un atteggiamento autoritario); in the political debates of 1797 'Venetian Pantaloons' (pantaloni veneti) and 'Pantaloons from the lagoons' (pantaloni delle lagune) are references to members of the oligarchy; a document from Palermo of 1799 mentions 'trousers termed Pantaloon style' (calzoni chiamati alla pantalona); and finally, the word appears in its modern sense in Foscolo (1809), Boerio (1829: 'Trousers in the fashion of sailors, that is long and wide, which cover the whole leg and became later quite a common apparel,' '*Calzoni alla marinaresca*, cioè Calzoni lunghi e larghi che ricuoprono tutta la gamba, e che poi passarono in uso presso che comune'), Manzoni, etc.

*Calzoni* appears earlier than *pantaloni*. It is found in Ariosto, Aretino, Bruno, and also in the sense of underpants in Della Casa.

It is an augmentative of *calza*, from the Latin *calceam*, *calceum* 'shoe' (see *calx* 'heel'). For present-day Italians who think they speak the language of Dante and Petrarch, the terms these poets used to designate the garment they wore around their legs may not come immediately to mind.

The dialect word in the Veneto is *braghe*, attested earlier than both *pantaloni* and *calzoni*. It derives from the Latin *bracae*, originally a Celtic word (or Germanic – possibly linked to *breeches*) for the clothing worn by the Gauls. The word *braca/braga* is documented in Latin (Lucilius 409: 'The Gauls abandoned the *bracae*, and donned the laticlave,' 'Galli bracas deposuerunt, latum clavum sumpserunt'); it is found in a papyrus from Ravenna of 564 (Tjäder 242); in a document of 721 in Du Cange; and in the vernacular *brague* in the twelfth century (Castellani), *braga e camixa* (breeches and shirt) in the thirteenth century (Monaci), and then from the fourteenth century on, in Giovanni Villani, Marco Polo volgare, Boccaccio, Burchiello, Aretino, Bruno, etc. It is also used in the sense of underpants, or *panni di gamba* (leg clothing) in Sacchetti. There is also the saying *calare le brache* for 'to concede defeat' (Salviati), the punning Tuscan proverb *A' sottili cascan le brache* (if you are too subtle/thin you'll lose your trousers), and in modern Italian the expression *rimanere* or *restare in braghe/brache di tela* (to be left high and dry), without any specifically regional connotation. To sum up: *braghe* today is undoubtedly a Venetian dialect word; but if it is used in an Italian sentence, one needs to establish whether it is an instance of popular Italian, an expressively appropriate borrowing from the dialect, or an ordinary Italian expression, perhaps a survival from Medieval Italian.

An Italian word for rubbish/refuse is *spazzatura* (or *spazzature*). It appears in a Latin document from Bologna of 1252 and then in Boccaccio (1353) and others. There are also other terms, such as *immondizia*, *immondizie* (Fra Giordano da Pisa, *Quaresimale fiorentino*, 1305–6; Boccaccio, etc.); *pattume*, from the end of the fourteenth century (from the Medieval Latin *pactume*, and see the modern *pattumiera* 'dustbin' in Tommaseo, Fanfani, etc.). Regionally, however, as frequently happens with everyday household terms, local dialectal expressions are preferred, such as those of the family of *rusco*, *rusca* in the Emilia region (of Celtic origin, documented in northern dialects from the thirteenth century; see *rusco* in Muratori). The dialect word in the Veneto region is *scoasse*. Battaglia gives *scoazzera 'recipiente per le spazzature'* (dustbin), from Boschini (1660), and *scovazze* from the sixteenth century (Girolamo Priuli's *Diari*, Pietro Nelli's *Satire*). If today one meets *scopacce*, how it is to be classified is not immediately obvious. To qualify these terms as 'popular' seems an oversimplification, and it appears that a little more caution would be welcome.

### 3.5. *Syntax*

In the area of syntax, too, the distinction between what is regional, locally familiar, colloquial and expressive, and what can be described as popular in the above sense, as revealing insufficient competence in the national language, is far from easily made. Here, again, I shall limit myself to discussing a few examples.

The first example is *a me mi piace* 'I like it,' which, as we have seen in section 2 above, can be considered almost a symbol, an icon of popular Italian, the sort of expression that is a mark of the semi-literate and that schoolteachers traditionally have had to correct in their pupils' works: in the literary language, *a me piace* or *mi piace* are the correct forms, and *a me mi piace* is wrong; it counts as a grammatical mistake and is therefore a characteristic example of popular Italian.

There is a sense in which this judgment is true, but only with certain provisos. In the first place, one has to consider the phenomenon of left dislocation, as in *questo libro l'ho già letto* (literally, 'this book I have already read it'). This usage is characteristic of the spoken language, but is largely documented in written Italian, in both the early and the modern period. (It even appears in the *Placito Capuano* of 960, the first dated vernacular document: *sao ko kelle terre ... trent'anni le possette* 'I know that those lands ... for thirty years were owned'.) It is less common in subsequent centuries, when a more formal, artificially constrained, Bembian literary standard prevailed. Left dislocation is not ungrammatical; its spoken connotation makes it suitable for an expressive, more lively usage in the literary language (see some examples from Boccaccio's *Decameron*, quoted in the study by Paolo D'Achille;[19] it is also found in sixteenth- and seventeenth-century Italian grammars, particularly when Spanish and Italian are contrasted; Edgar Radtke, in a 1987 article, even suggested that *a me mi piace* was occasionally considered standard in the Seicento[20]).

There is a further complicating factor, however, which makes the interpretation of *a me mi piace* as a case of left dislocation rather problematic. While *questo libro l'ho già letto* and its counterparts in the dialects are optional structures, side by side with *ho già letto questo libro*, the pattern of *a me mi piace* is, in most if not all Italian dialects, compulsory (as it is in Spanish; see Cortelazzo's 1984 article: 'Perché "a mi me gusta" sì e "a me mi piace" no?'[21]). An expression such as *a me piace* is simply not available in Italian dialects, and whereas one can meet any number of literary examples of left dislocation of the *questo libro l'ho già letto* type, instances of the *a me mi piace* type seem more difficult to find.

An example comes to mind from Carducci, but it is a case of right, rather than left, dislocation. Also, it is uttered not by a human but by an animal. In the poem from *Rime Nuove*, with the title *Il passo di Roncisvalle* (a translation from Spanish and Portuguese romances), the father of Don Beltran is sent to find the body of his son killed in battle. He says he does not want to blame for his death either the Christians or the infidels: he'll blame the horse instead, which was not able to keep Don Beltran out of danger and bring him back safely: 'But the steed who was half dead / Thus began he to speak out: / -Me, don't lay the blame on me / That I could not bring him back' (Il cavallo mezzo morto / Così prese a favellar: / -Non mi dare a me la colpa / Che no'l seppi ritornar; ll. 107–10). I am not sure whether this implies that for Carducci animals speak popular Italian, or that popular Italian is an idiom fit for animals.

To satisfy my curiosity, I looked up Carducci's sources.[22] They are two Spanish romances: 'En los campos de Aluentosa' (also translated by Berchet, in his *Vecchie romanze spagnuole*, 1837), and 'Por la matança va el viejo'; the third source is Portuguese: 'Quedos, quedos, cavaleiros.' When we look at the three original romances, we find that it is only in the Portuguese version that the horse speaks to defend itself, but without using a reduplicated pronoun. In the Spanish one, 'En los campos de Aluentosa,' it is instead a Moor who takes the defence of the horse. We may observe that Berchet, in his translation, uses a left dislocation, but not a double pronoun as Carducci does: 'Al caval non gli dar colpa: / dargli colpa staria mal'; and in the original Spanish: 'no le des culpa al cauallo / que no se la puedes dar.'

In any case, the idea that *a me mi piace* is a straight transfer of a dialect feature into the standard and, as such, an awkward regionalism rather than simply an accepted expressive device, needs at least to be considered. Whether people who use it are ipso facto revealing insufficient familiarity with the standard, as the reference to popular Italian would suggest, is, of course, a different matter. It seems to me that an expression such as *a me queste cose non mi piacciono* is as likely to be uttered (and even to be used in writing, in an appropriate context) by speakers of standard Italian as by speakers of popular Italian.

Another example that illustrates the difficulty of discriminating between standard and popular Italian is found in the use of the accusative forms for subject pronouns. It is clear that *lui/lei* are fully accepted in the spoken standard, as subjects, in preference to *egli/ella, essa.* In the written standard there are textual conditions in which *egli/ella, essa* are required, when the pronoun has an anaphoric rather than a deictic function.

For the first and second person the conditions vary according to the region. *Me* and *te* used as subjects, in the north seem to belong to popular Italian (corresponding to dialect forms *mi* and *ti*): *me dico che, te dici che,* and so on do not belong to the standard, spoken or written, for a northern speaker. For the first person, the same applies to Tuscan speakers, but for the second person, *te,* used as subject, belongs to Tuscan usage ([te] with a closed [e], not [tɛ] with an open [ɛ], as in the north). As we saw above for the use of ['ma:ʒiko], the historical link between Tuscan usage and the standard prevents one from classifying *te lo sai che,* or *ci pensi te?* as popular Italian, since they are used by Tuscan speakers who are fully familiar with the literary standard. In fact, forms such as *io e te* have been prescribed by Italian school grammars for generations. (Note that one is taught to use *io e te,* not *io e tu,* but *tu ed io,* not *te ed io,* notwithstanding Tuscan usage.)

## 4. *Conclusion*
If we now try to draw some tentative conclusions, I think that we can say the following.

(a) The notion of popular Italian, elaborated explicitly in the 1960s and 1970s, arose in the context of a useful and valiant attempt to deal with a period, covering the first century after unification, in which to the two different systems (that of written, literary Italian, used by an educated minority, and that of the spoken dialects, differing according to region, used in speech by everyone, literate or illiterate) a third system was added, that of spoken Italian, which, under the pressure of the standard from above and of the dialects from below, found it difficult to establish its autonomy, and, particularly in its written manifestations, in the hands of the semiliterate acquired the reputation of a substandard idiom, characteristic of the uneducated. This is what is normally meant by popular Italian.

(b) The situation changed during the second half of the twentieth century, however, particularly owing to the overwhelming diffusion of television in the 1950s and 1960s. For the first time in history the Italian population was in daily contact with a spoken language, used in the same way throughout the country. People born after 1950 could acquire Italian (rather than a dialect) as a mother tongue (see above, chapter one, section 3.5). It is difficult to overestimate the importance of this change, which is ongoing. Whether the impact of the electronic age – email, computer, mobile phones, and so on – will be comparable and how it will affect Italian usage is still to be clarified. (Recently, I have seen some studies on the SMS, an acronym for 'short message service,' in Italian 'messaggini.'[23]) A third system, that of ordinary Italian, both spoken and written, is replacing the two previous ones, that is, that of the literary language (used mainly in writing) and that of the dialects (used mainly in speech). This third system, which I have called 'ordinary Italian,' has, in a sense, succeeded popular Italian but lost the substandard connotations of the latter. It is no longer the sort of language used by dialect speakers who have learnt Italian imperfectly. Modern ordinary Italian can actually be defined as the language used by Italians, who often are not native speakers of a dialect and who also may not be competent users of the literary idiom. From this viewpoint Italian has become similar to other languages, such as English, French, or German. This suggests not a rigorously unified and standardized system, but a mobile and flexible one, which allows for regional, social, situational, and individual variation.

Going back to our original question – fact or fiction? – we could say that if popular Italian was in some sense a fiction, modern Italian has become a fact, in a way comparable to that in which other European languages are facts. In other words, Italian can now be called 'popular,' not in the sense of being used by the uneducated, but of being (or being in the process of becoming) the everyday language of the whole population.

NOTES

1 For an introduction see Giulio Lepschy, 'L'italiano popolare: Riflessioni su riflessioni,' *L'Italia linguistica: Idee, storia, strutture*, ed. Federico Albano Leoni et al. (Bologna: il Mulino, 1983), 269–82; also in Lepschy, *Nuovi saggi di linguistica italiana* (Bologna: il Mulino, 1989), 37–50.

2 Henri Bauche, *Le Langage populaire* (Paris: Payot, 1920; 2nd ed., 1951).

3 Pierre Guiraud, *Le Français populaire* (Paris: PUF, 1963).

4 Maurice Grevisse, *Le Bon usage* (Gembloux: Duculot, 1936).

5 Hermann Wunderlich, *Unsere Umgangssprache* [sic] *in der Eigenart ihrer Satzfügung dargestellt* (Weimar and Berlin: Felber, 1894).

6 See also the important volume on Latin by Johann Baptist Hofman, *Lateinische Umgangssprache* (Heidelberg: Winter, 1926); Italian translation by Licinia Ricottilli, *La lingua d'uso latina* (Bologna: Patron, 1980).

7 Leo Spitzer, *Italienische Umgangssprache* (Bonn and Leipzig: Schroeder, 1922).

8 Leo Spitzer, *Italienische Kriegsgefangenenbriefe* (Bonn: Hanstein, 1921); Italian edition, *Lettere di prigionieri di guerra italiani, 1915–1918* (Turin: Boringhieri, 1976), with a 'Nota linguistica' by Laura Vanelli, 295–312.

9 Peter Trudgill, 'On the Limits of Passive "Competence": Sociolinguistics and the Polylectal Grammar Controversy,' in *Linguistic Controversies: Essays in*

*Linguistic Theory and Practice in Honour of F. R. Palmer*, ed. David Crystal (London: Arnold, 1982), 172–91.

10  See Gaetano Berruto, 'La natura linguistica dell'italiano popolare,' in *Varietätenlinguistik des Italienischen*, ed. Günter Holtus and Edgar Radtke (Tübingen: Narr, 1983), 86–106; Berruto, *Sociolinguistica dell'italiano contemporaneo* (Florence: La Nuova Italia Scientifica, 1987); Berruto, 'Varietà diamesiche, diastratiche, diafasiche,' in *Introduzione all'italiano contemporaneo: La variazione e gli usi*, ed. Alberto A. Sobrero (Rome and Bari: Laterza, 1993), 37–92; Francesco Bruni, *L'italiano nelle regioni: Lingua nazionale e identità regionali* (Turin: UTET, 1992); Michele A. Cortelazzo, *Italiano d'oggi* (Padua: Esedra, 2000); Paolo D'Achille, 'L'italiano dei semicolti,' in *Storia della lingua italiana*, vol. 2. *Scritto e parlato*, ed. Luca Serianni and Pietro Trifone (Turin: Einaudi, 1994), 41–79; Gerhard Ernst, 'Existiert ein "italiano popolare unitario"?' in *Italienische Sprachwissenschaft*, ed. Christoph Schwarze (Tübingen: Narr, 1981), 99–113; Pier Vincenzo Mengaldo, *'Il Novecento,'* in *Storia della lingua italiana*, ed. Francesco Bruni (Bologna: il Mulino, 1994); Arturo Tosi, *Language and Society in a Changing Italy* (Clevedon: Multilingual Matters, 2001).

11  Anna Laura Lepschy and Giulio Lepschy, 'La situazione dell'italiano,' in *La linguistica italiana degli anni 1976–1986*, Pubblicazioni della SLI, 31, ed. Alberto M. Mioni and Michele A. Cortelazzo (Rome: Bulzoni, 1992), 27–37.

12  Francesco Sabatini, 'L'italiano dell'uso medio: una realtà tra le varietà linguistiche italiane,' in *Gesprochenes Italienisch in Geschichte und Gegenwart*, ed. Günter Holtus and Edgar Radtke (Tübingen: Narr, 1985), 154–84.

13  Tullio De Mauro, 'Per lo studio dell'italiano popolare unitario,' in Annabella Rossi, *Lettere da una tarantata* (Bari: De Donato, 1970), 43–75; also in *La lingua italiana oggi: un problema scolastico e sociale*, ed. Lorenzo Renzi and Michele A. Cortelazzo (Bologna: il Mulino, 1977), 147–64. Manlio Cortelazzo, *Lineamenti di italiano popolare* (Pisa: Pacini, 1972).

14  Tullio De Mauro, *Grande dizionario italiano dell'uso* (Turin: UTET: 1999).

15  Tullio De Mauro, *Storia linguistica dell'Italia unita* (Bari: Laterza, 1963).

16  For texts in popular Italian see Giovanni Rovere, *Testi di italiano popolare: Autobiografie di lavoratori e figli di lavoratori emigrati* (Rome: Centro Studi Emigrazione, 1977); Francesco Bruni, *L'italiano nelle regioni: Testi e documenti* (Turin: UTET, 1994).

17  For current presentations of the norm, from different points of view, see Anna Laura Lepschy and Giulio Lepschy, *The Italian Language Today* (London:

Hutchinson, 1977; new ed. London: Routledge, 1991); Francesco Bruni, *L'italiano: Elementi di storia della lingua e della cultura* (Turin: UTET, 1984); Luca Serianni, in collaboration with Alberto Castelvecchi, *Grammatica italiana: Italiano comune, lingua letteraria: Suoni forme costrutti* (Turin: UTET, 1988); Martin Maiden, *A Linguistic History of Italian* (London and New York: Longman, 1995), Italian translation, *Storia linguistica dell'italiano* (Bologna: il Mulino, 1998); Gianrenzo P. Clivio and Marcel Danesi, *The Sounds, Forms and Uses of Italian: An Introduction to Italian Linguistics* (Toronto: University of Toronto Press, 2000); Martin Maiden and Cecilia Robustelli, *A Reference Grammar of Modern Italian* (London: Arnold, 2000).

19 The earliest known mention of Pantalone seems to be in a letter written by Stefano Guazzo in 1561; Guazzo also mentions, in 1586, people 'masked in the dress of Pantaloni' ('mascherati in habito di Pantaloni'). See Giovanni Presa, 'Pantalone,' *Lingua nostra* 40 (1979), 55.

19 Paolo D'Achille, *Sintassi del parlato e tradizione scritta della lingua italiana: Analisi di testi dalle origini al secolo XVIII* (Rome: Bonacci, 1990), 105–7.

20 Edgar Radtke, '*A me mi piace* als Standardform im Seicento,' *Zeitschrift für romanische Philologie* 103 (1987), 370–88; see also Radtke, 'Bestimmungskriterien für das italiano popolare,' in *Italienische Sprachwissenschaft*, ed. Christoph Schwarze (Tubingen: Narr, 1981), 147–57.

21 Manlio Cortelazzo, 'Perché "a mí me gusta" sì e "a me mi piace" no?' in *Umgangssprache in der Iberoromania*, ed. Günter Holtus and Edgar Radtke (Tubingen: Narr, 1984), 25–8.

22 He mentions them in an article in *Nuova Antologia* ser. 2, vol. 27 (May–June 1881), 241.

23 See Michele Cortelazzo, 'Telefonini cellulari e computer rilanciano la scrittura ideografica,' *Telèma* 23 (2000–1), 102–4.

# CHAPTER FOUR

# Secondary Stress: Surface Contrasts

In sections 1–5 of this chapter[1] some observations will be made on the study of stress levels, with particular reference to Italian. In sections 6 and 7 a correlation will be identified between (a) three kinds of word structure, that is, (i) compounds ending in a free form, (ii) compounds ending in a bound form, (iii) simple and derived words, and (b) three corresponding different patterns of stress levels.

To some of these questions I have returned repeatedly, at extended intervals, during the last forty years, starting with a 1957 B.A. dissertation on the problem of the Latin accent,[2] and proceeding to studies of stress and intonation in Italian,[3] and to an examination of Italian secondary stress.[4] Relevant theories have evolved dramatically during this period, from Chomsky, Halle, and Lukoff,[5] to Chomsky and Halle,[6] to the elaboration of prosodic and metrical phonology, to the representational analysis put forward by optimality theory.[7] On the other hand, it should be noted that my encounters with these hypotheses occurred mostly in the context of my interest in the analysis of Italian. In this chapter, too, I shall concentrate on some low-level (but in my view not banal) factual questions, rather than on theoretical ones. There is, of course, a distinction, not a conflict, between work that deals with theory (the facts being interesting insofar as they can confirm or contradict theoretical hypotheses) and work that attempts to establish and in some way reasonably account for facts (rather than their relevance from the viewpoint of a given theoretical framework).

## 1. *The Study of Stress Levels*

When I was a student, a common question concerned the number of levels of stress that were necessary to account for ordinary usage in, say, English or in Italian. The question was often linked, in an impressionistic way, to the distinction between a phonetic and a phonemic point of view. It was generally accepted that in terms of phonetic realization one could have a gradient, with different syllables exhibiting indefinitely varying levels of prominence, which a narrow transcription could represent with a degree of precision depending on how gifted or well trained one was as a practical phonetician. It was also assumed that one's transcription could be confirmed instrumentally by traces produced by a machine or images appearing on a monitor. Confidence, however, was sometimes undermined by specialists in acoustics who pointed out that intensity and perceived loudness were different and that establishing the physical correlates of stress was not a completely straightforward operation.

Even though the relation between phonetic and phonemic was not unproblematic, it was generally assumed that the indefinite variation of phonetic realizations could be reduced to a small number of phonemic units, which were supposed to be clearly perceivable and identifiable. In the area of suprasegmentals linguists described a system of four pitch phonemes, and a parallel one of four stress phonemes. The assumption was that, both for English and for Italian, a system of four degrees of stress was necessary and sufficient in order to account for the different degrees of accentual prominence perceived in speech. Bloch and Trager recorded four contrasting grades of stress, transcribed as follows, from loudest to weakest, with marks over the vowel (the weakest being represented by the absence of a mark): *á, â, à, a*, as in *cúrrent, cóntènts, bláck-bîrd, ôld-mán, élevàtor-ôperàtor.*[8] Agard and Di Pietro use four degrees of stress for Italian: a strong (´) and an intermediate (`) one, as in *pòrtabagágli*; a weak one for unstressed syllables, which can be left unmarked; and a movable one (˝), which represents the strongest level and forms the centre of an intonational structure.[9]

It is interesting to note that, in the tradition of European phonology, pitch and stress were sharply separated according to their function.[10] Martinet observed that while a tone is an oppositive, paradigmatic entity, which can be identified even in the absence of contrasting entities within the same segment (one can have a monosyllabic utterance containing only one tone), stress is a contrastive, syntagmatic entity, which can only be identified in relation to a preceding or following unit of the same nature.[11] The stressed first syllable *fi-* of the Italian word *fini* (ends) is recognized as stressed, owing to its contrast with the following unstressed syllable *-ni*, and is not opposed to (in fact, it is indistinguishable from) the unstressed *fi-* of *finì* (past definite of *finire*). The opposition is therefore not between the *fi-* of *fini* and the *fi-* of *finì*, but between the trochaic stress pattern /– ∪/ of *fini* and the iambic one /∪ –/ of *finì*. This explanation may, in fact, be misleading, since it is reasonable to assume that if one were to isolate, in a recording, the segments corresponding to the initial syllables of *fini* and of *finì*, and listen to those two first syllables in isolation, they would be distinguishable, owing to length and pitch differences. They appear to be identical in the metalinguistic situation in which they are 'mentioned,' and thus one has the two homophonous words *fi*, that is, the names of the first syllables of *fini* and *finì*, carrying the stress and tone that are required by the sentence in which they are used as words; for instance: '*fi-* is the first syllable of the word *fini*,' and '*fi-* is the first syllable of the word *finì*.'

There is little point, therefore, in trying to identify four different stress phonemes, or four kinds of stressed syllables. There is only one 'stress' (as was pointed out in a memorable article by Chomsky, Halle, and Lukoff[12]) that is assigned to minimum relevant units and, through a complex system of rules or by using grids or trees, it leads to a surface representation in which the appropriate degrees of prominence are manifested.

## 2. *Secondary Prominence*

These proposals can be looked at in a more general context, which includes a reconsideration of phonological principles, as in Halle's *The Sound Pattern of Russian*, in which the notion of a phonemic level is rejected and replaced with the derivational history that links abstract structures of a morphophonemic nature to surface phonetic realizations.[13] However, one needs to deal with the fact that certain stress patterns are perceived as being distinct from others. It seems to me that there is no incompatibility between, on the one hand, proposing that only one stress is assigned to each relevant unit (say, to each word or formative), with compositional rules accounting for the resulting degrees of prominence of different syllables; and, on the other hand, trying to establish how many distinctive levels of prominence are perceived in any individual stretch of speech.

One may want to interpret the word *portabagagli* as simply having two main stresses, one on *-ga-* and one on *por-*. Doing so, however, does not alter the fact that *-ga-* has greater prominence than *por-*, and that the other three syllables are even less prominent and can be described as being equally unstressed, or perhaps exhibiting different levels of weak prominence.

It has been suggested (in Fudge, from which we adapt the following example)[14] that people are unable to discriminate between more than three levels of prominence (apart from a fourth level, for unstressed syllables). For simple words (but not for complex words or phrases) it seems sufficient to record a main stress ('in front of the syllable), a secondary stress (` in front of the syllable), and lack of stress (no mark). In a phrase such as *elevator operator training scheme*, individual words can be marked as follows: *('ele`vator) ('ope`rator) ('training) ('scheme)*; if we build our structure by adding (on the left of the existing stress mark) a main stress to one constituent and a secondary stress to the other, as appropriate, at the next step we get: *("ele`vator `'ope`rator) ("training `'scheme)*; and at the final one: *("'ele`vator `'ope`rator `"training `'scheme)*. But the four hierarchical levels (''', `'', `', `) plus one for unstressed syllables, resulting from the constituent structure of the phrase, would be reduced, in a phonetic transcription based on perceived prominence, to three degrees of stress (",',,), plus one, unmarked, for unstressed syllables: "*ele,vator ,ope,rator 'training ,scheme*.

An equivalent Italian example is *corso addestramento nuovi neolaureati*, in which syllabic prominence can be represented as follows: *('corso) (addestra'mento) ('nuovi) (`neolaure'ati)*; we are introducing a secondary degree of prominence on *neo-* (see section 7 below). At the successive levels we find: *(`'corso addestra"mento) (`'nuovi `neolaure"ati), (`'corso addestra`'mento `nuovi `neolaure'''ati)*, and using the traditional vertical bars: ,*corso addestra'mento ,nuovi ,neolaure"ati*.

It may be useful to recall that, in the first edition (1917) of the *English Pronouncing Dictionary* by Daniel Jones, two marks were used, one for 'strong stress' (' above the line), and one for 'secondary stress' (` below the line).[15] Since the fourth (1937) edition they have been replaced by the customary vertical bars above and below the line. In the fourteenth edition, edited by A.C. Gimson, we read that 'there is one exceptional case when the rule of only one sign ' per word has been relaxed. Long polysyllabic words or compounds have *two* secondary stresses preceding the primary. Of the secondary stresses, the first is the stronger (while remaining subsidiary to the primary)' and it is marked with the same vertical bar as the primary stress (*'indi,visi'bility*), with the understanding that it represents, however, a weaker stress.[16] In the fifteenth edition the rule of giving one primary stress per word was applied consistently.[17] The editors accept that an argument can be made for recognizing a tertiary stress, in words such as *indivisibility*, but they choose to mark it in the same way as a secondary stress (hence *,indi,visi'bility*), bearing in mind that the second one is weaker than the first. In the *Longman Pronunciation Dictionary* J. Wells also recognizes three degrees of stress and represents the tertiary one with a circle below the line (*,indi₀visi'bility*).[18] The prevailing opinion seems to be that, in fact, one needs to consider four levels: three for stressed syllables (primary, secondary, tertiary) and one for unstressed (with the possibility of further distinguishing strong vowels from weak vowels in unstressed syllables). In the Italian word *indivisibilità* one can also distinguish four levels, marking a primary stress on the last syllable, a secondary on the first, a tertiary on the fourth, and leaving unmarked (unstressed) the second, third, fifth, and sixth: *,indivi₀sibili'tà*. Italian secondary stress will be discussed below.

## 3. *Italian Stress*

While for English there are a substantial number of studies on stress placement,[19] for Italian the bibliography seems to be less satisfactory.[20] Traditional accounts of Italian stress seem to fall back on the Latin trisyllabic conditions requiring words to be stressed on one of the last three syllables.[21] Normally, words can be 'piane' (paroxytonic: *vedere, calore*), 'tronche' (oxytonic: *bontà, però*), or 'sdrucciole' (proparoxytonic: *prendere, tavola*). Long words can be 'bisdrucciole' (*caricano*) or, with the addition of clitics, carry a stress even further away from the end, on the fifth (*caricamelo, caricamici*), sixth (*caricamicelo*), and so on.

Concerning secondary stress, traditional accounts tend to distinguish between pretonic and post-tonic syllables. For post-tonic syllables it has been suggested that a final syllable has a secondary stress and is, in turn, preceded by secondarily stressed syllables at intervals of one, but no secondary stress can be immediately preceded by a main stress. Such a system allows for the following patterns (marking main stress with an acute accent and secondary with a grave accent): *caricáre*, *cáricà*, *cáricanò*, *cáricàmelò*, *cáricamìcelò*, and so forth. This account of the situation seems to be reasonably accurate. Note, however, that according to Vogel and Scalise, there is no secondary prominence on post-tonics.[22]

For pretonic syllables the situation seems to be more varied. Traditional descriptions refer to the placement of secondary stresses (a) to the left of the main stress, at alternate intervals, as in *divìnitá*, *òpportùnitá*; or (b) on the initial syllable, as in *dìvinitá*, *òccidentále*. According to Bertinetto, however, instrumental analysis appears to assign greater prominence to the syllable immediately preceding the tonic.[23] This observation contradicts the intuitive notion of stressability, which suggests patterns such as *dìnamíte*, *lìbertá*, *òpportùnitá*.

## 4. Italian Secondary Stress (Vogel and Scalise)

An influential account of secondary stress in Italian is offered by Vogel and Scalise; they make use of four general rules: (a) avoidance of stress in adjacent syllables: *occidént+ále* > *occidentále*; (b) introduction of secondary stress on the first syllable: *occidentále* > *òccidentále*; (c) stress reversal: *divìnitá* > *dìvinitá*; (d) insertion of secondary stress into stretches of more than two unstressed syllables: *rìnocerontíno* > *rìnocèrontíno*. Vogel and Scalise also identified what they called a 'small group' of words subject to variable accentual patterns: exhibiting (i) a trochaic pattern, apparently common in northern Italy, as in *càrattèrizzábile*, *còmunìcazióne*, *èlettrìcitá*, *èncefàlográmma, gènerìcaménte*; (ii) an iambic pattern, apparently common in southern Italy, as in *caràtterizzábile, comùnicazióne, elèttricitá, encèfalográmma, genèricaménte*. It also seems that pattern (i) is more common with familiar words, such as *èlettricitá*, and pattern (ii) with unfamiliar words, such as *encèfalográmma*. Words following pattern (ii) may undergo stress reversal and (against rule [d] above) surface as *càratterizzábile, còmunicazióne, èlettricitá, gènericaménte*.[25]

Finally, these generalizations apply to simple and derived words, but compounds may contradict them by exhibiting (a) adjacency of stresses, as in *blù nótte*; (b)-(c) secondary stress on the second rather than the first syllable, as in *aspìrapólvere*; (d) stretches of more than two unstressed syllables, as in *màcina caffé, càrcere modéllo*.

## 5. *Italian Secondary Stress (Peperkamp)*

An interesting recent discussion of secondary stress has been offered by Sharon Peperkamp. This contribution presents a critical analysis of current bibliography and proposes an account that is not rule based but representational, that is, in the context of optimality theory it relies on a system of constraints on representation. These constraints affect metrical structure: (a) feet must be binary and in Italian trochaic; (b) alignment: the left edge of a prosodic word must coincide with the left edge of a foot; (c) alignment: a morphological word must begin with a foot; (d) parsing: syllables must be dominated by feet; (e) metrical consistency: morphemes must surface with their underlying stress. Constraints are hierarchically ranked, and their ranking is language specific. Peperkamp argues that the generalizations of Vogel and Scalise would lend themselves to a more coherent, principled formulation if presented in terms of the ranked system of constraints of optimality theory. This may well be the case. What concerns us more directly in this chapter is the discussion of some data at a more elementary, factual level.[26]

## 6. *Italian Secondary Stress (Lepschy)*

### 6.1. *Marking Secondary Stress*
In the course of work for a major new dictionary,[27] it was suggested[28] that it would be useful to mark (contrary to traditional lexicographical practice) secondary stresses in the phonetic transcription, for all the words in which their presence was distinctive. We tried to formulate (profiting also from discussions with Tullio De Mauro) some instructions that could be applied without too many uncertainties by the compilers of the dictionary. In the rest of this article we shall present the situation as we see it. First, we should make three sets of distinctions, as indicated in 6.2, 6.3, and 6.4.

### 6.2. *Word Structure*
For our purpose, words can be put into one of three groups, according to whether they are

(1) compounds that end in an independent word (free form), for example, *portafinestra, portaombrelli*;
(2) compounds that end in a non-independent word (bound form), for example, *farmacologia, etruscologia*;
(3) simple or derived words, for example, *opportunità, caratterizzabile, indivisibilità*.

In group (1), compounds may have a free form or a bound form as a non-final component, as in *spremilimoni* and *paleomarxista*, respectively. What counts as a final free form may itself be a composite formative ending in a bound form, for example, *fonomorfo-*

*logia*, interpreted as (fono)+(morfologia), rather than as (fono-morfo)+(logia).

In group (2), the final component is a bound form, and the preceding component may also be a bound form, as in *omofono*. In cases like *farmacologia, etruscologia*, one may wonder whether the pre-final component is a free form (*farmaco, etrusco*) or, as seems more likely, a bound form ending in a linking vowel *-o* (as in *morfologia*). These forms involve components that seem to have greater autonomy and semantic weight than prefixes or suffixes. These components were called by Migliorini 'prefixoids' and 'suffixoids'[29] and more recently have been designated as 'semi-words.' The resulting structures have been considered in terms sometimes of derivation,[30] sometimes of composition.[31]

Group (3) includes two kinds of words, simple and derived. The distinction is not clear-cut and straightforward, since it seems to rely on whether certain words are felt to result from a productive, synchronic process of derivation. But how far one can go in analysing the structure of a word, from a synchronic viewpoint, depends on a judgment that may vary from individual to individual and from word to word: *impossibile* and *intrepido*, *premettere* and *preservare* might be felt by some speakers (but not by others) to be synchronically derived forms in all cases, or in none, or in two cases (*impossibile, premettere*), but not in the others (*intrepido, preservare*).

As for the difference between prefixes and suffixes, we may observe that the former tend not to change the category of the word (*mettere* vs *immettere, premettere*), while the latter may (*premettere* vs *premessa*), or may not (*mettere* vs *mettendo*) do so.

Prefixes and prefixoids seem to enjoy greater prosodic autonomy than suffixes and suffixoids and to be more relevant to our present interests, since it is normally right-hand formatives that carry the main stress, while a secondary degree of prominence tends to appear on left-hand formatives.

### 6.3. *Placement of Secondary Prominence*

Syllables with a secondary degree of prominence will be indicated by writing their vowels in capitals. Main stress (primary prominence) will be marked with an acute accent. As far as the position of the syllables with secondary prominence is concerned, one should distinguish four possibilities:

(A) Anatony: we shall call this position 'anatonic' with reference to the original position of the main stress when the formative is used as an independent word: *cristAllo-chímica, cOmico-irónico, fArmacología, papIrología, cristAllografía, Avidaménte, abusIvaménte, opportUnitá.*

(B) Prototony: we shall call 'prototonic' the placement of the secondary degree of prominence on the first syllable (when this does not correspond to the original main stress of the formative used as an independent word, in which case secondary prominence on the first syllable would be anatonic): *pApirología, crIstallografía, Abusivaménte, Opportunitá, cAratterízzo, cAratterizzáre, cAratterizzabilíssimo.*

(C) Deuterotony: we shall call 'deuterotonic' the placement of the secondary degree of prominence on the second syllable (when this does not correspond to the original main stress of the formative used as an independent word, in which case secondary prominence on the second syllable would be anatonic): *avIdaménte, stupIdaménte, abUsivaménte, oppOrtunitá.*

(D) Polytony: we shall call 'polytonic' the placement of a secondary degree of prominence on two or more syllables of the left-hand formative. This is the result of combining (B) with those cases of (A) in which the secondary prominence is on the third syllable; and (B) or (C) with those cases of (A) in which the secondary prominence is on the fourth or following syllable, as in

A (on the third syllable) + B: *AbusIvaménte, AbbarbAgliaménto, OpportUnitá, prOnunciAbilitá*;
A (on the fourth syllable) + B: *prOvvidenziAlitá*;
A (on the fourth syllable) + C: *provvIdenziAlitá*;
A (on the fifth syllable) + B: *cAratterizzAbilitá, cAratterizzAbilíssimo*;
A (on the fifth syllable) + C: *carAtterizzAbilitá, carAtterizzAbilíssimo*.

### 6.4. Secondary Prominence and Word Structure

The distinctions made in 6.2 and those made in 6.3 seem to be related in an interesting way.

In words belonging to group 1, secondary prominence can be only of type A: *tEsta-códa, pOrta-finéstra, pOrtacénere, cristAllochímica, cOmico-irónico*. We cannnot find type B (*\*crIstallochímica*), or C (*\*comIco-irónico*), or D (*\*cAratterizzAbilitÀ-comprensibilitá, \*carAtterizzabilitÀ-comprensibilitá*).

In words belonging to group 2, secondary prominence can be of type A (*fArmacología, etrUscología, vitamInología*), or of type B (*Etruscología, vItaminología*). We do not find type C (*\*farmAcología, \*vitAminología*), or D involving C (*\*naziOnalIsmofobía*); we can find type D as long as it involves B (*vItamInofobía*).

In words belonging to group 3, secondary prominence can be of type A (*cAricherébbero, Avidaménte; carAtterístico, divInitá; abusIvaménte, opportUnitá, pronunciAbilitá; provvidenziAlitá; caratterizzAbilitá*), or of type B (*cAratterístico, dIvinitá, Abusivaménte, Opportunitá, prOnunciabilitá, prOvvidenzialitá*), or of type C (*carIcherébbero, avIdaménte, abUsivaménte, oppOrtunitá, pronUnciabilitá, provvIdenzialitá*), or of type D (*AbusIvaménte, prOvvidenziAlitá, provvIdenziAlitá, cAratterizzAbilitá, carAtterizzAbilitá*).

## 6.5. *Relation between Word Structure and Secondary Prominence*

In section 6.4 we highlighted a significant correlation between the data presented in 6.2 and in 6.3. In 6.2 we classified words into three groups according to their morphological structure: the degree of autonomy and the semantic weight of the individual formatives seem progressively to diminish as we proceed from group 1 (words that are clearly compounds, in which the final component can function as an independent word and carries the main stress), to group 2 (compounds in which the fusion between the formatives is stronger, their semantic identity is less clear-cut, and the final component cannot function as an independent word), and finally to group 3 (words that are not compounds and in which the identification of the formatives is less straightforward).

Conversely, from the viewpoint of prosody, the placement of secondary prominence seems to be subject to a strict rule for words of group 1 (type A: secondary prominence can only appear on those syllables, in the left-hand formative, which would have the main stress if the formative were independent). It has a progressively increasing degree of freedom in group 2 (secondary prominence can be of type A or B, i.e., on the originally stressed syllable, and, for each word in which this was not the first, there is an alternative pronunciation with secondary prominence on the first syllable). This freedom is even more pronounced in group 3, in which we find words having an array of alternative pronunciations, with secondary prominence not only on the syllable that was originally stressed (type A), but also on the first (type B), or second (type C), or on more than one syllable (type D), combining the three possibilities mentioned above.

Only in the words belonging to group 1 does secondary prominence occupy a fixed position, on a predetermined syllable in the left-hand formative; and, crucially, only in words belonging to group 1, is the opposition between mid-high [e] [o] and mid-low [ɛ] [ɔ] preserved in syllables that have secondary prominence. In words belonging to groups 2 and 3 this opposition is neutralized. Thus, syllables with secondary prominence behave as if they were stressed in group 1 and as if they were unstressed in groups 2 and 3.

It is suggested that we adopt the following terminological and notational convention. We shall talk about primary, secondary, and so on degrees of prominence on a more impressionistic level, for groups 2 and 3, and of main and secondary stresses only with reference to the accentual patterns of compounds in group 1. When using ordinary spelling we shall mark secondary prominence with capital letters and main and secondary stresses with an acute and a grave accent, respectively. If necessary the phonetic symbols [e] [ɛ] [o] [ɔ] can be inserted into conventional spelling: *p*[ɔ]*rta-fin*[ɛ]*stra*. In phonetic transcription we shall use the traditional vertical bars, superscript for main stress, subscript for secondary stress. If necessary, a tertiary degree of prominence can be marked by a subscript circle, as indicated above.

It may be useful, at least for Italian, to designate a secondary degree of prominence (which does not have the phonological value of the secondary stress we attribute to words of group 1) with a different term, such as 'rhythmic stress.'[32] The capital letters used for secondary prominence allow us to ignore the opposition between mid-high and mid-low vowels, in the tradition of Trubeckoj's use of capital letters for archiphonemes.

In De Mauro's dictionary an attempt has been made to use secondary stresses systematically for all words belonging to group 1.[33] This procedure, however, cannot be applied mechanically and in a straightforward way. In the following section some of the questions will be mentioned that arise in ascribing words to group 1 and analysing them. The pronunciation of these words and the judgment of whether two expressions are homophonous or phonologically distinct may vary from speaker to speaker. Even in cases involving the opposition between open and closed *e*s and *o*s (preserved under secondary stress, neutralized under secondary prominence and in unstressed syllables) one needs to keep in mind that there are regional (and indeed even individual) varieties in which (a) the distribution of open and closed *e*s and *o*s within specific words differs from that of the Tuscan norm; (b) the opposition may be absent (or may be determined by the phonological context) for one, or both, of these vowels; (c) the realization of secondary stress/prominence may vary according to intonational and contextual factors. In this chapter we are referring to the pronunciation of individual words in isolation, in the style adopted by speakers offering the pronunciation of a lexical entry, a lemma in a dictionary. The considerations that follow are based on our own reactions and those of native Italian friends, colleagues, and students we have consulted. There has been no attempt to gather statistical data; they would certainly have their own use, but we feel they would not affect the comments presented here, which are based on our own intuitions.

## 7. Secondary Stress vs Secondary Prominence

### 7.1. Compounds vs Single or Derived Words

Group 1 vs group 3. A word may be interpreted as fitting into the pattern of compounds (group 1, with secondary stress), or taken as an undivided unit (group 3, with secondary prominence), depending on factors such as familiarity, frequency, the phonological wear-and-tear, so to speak, that obstructs its analysability. In a word like *portacappelli* we expect to hear and we use the pronunciation *p*[ɔ]*rtacappélli*, but in *portafogli* (or *portafoglio*) we often hear and we use *pOrtafógli* (or *pOrtafóglio*). In the former case the word refers to a rarely used object in which hats can be carried; in the latter case the word means 'wallet' and does not convey the idea of an object used to carry around sheets of paper. Some speakers say p[ɔ]rtafógli, the secondary stress corresponding to the pattern of compounds belonging to group 1, but this does not necessarily mean that their semantic interpretation of the word is different from that of speakers who pronounce it as if it belonged to group 3.

### 7.2. *Free vs Bound Forms*

Group 1 vs group 2. A word such as *paleografico* can have two pronunciations and, accordingly, two interpretations. The ordinary pronunciation, following the pattern of group 2, is *pAleográfico*, referring to paleography: it is an adjective derived from *paleografia*, a term in which the last formative is *-grafia*, rather than the independent word *grafia*. It is the word for a discipline (the study of ancient writing), not for ancient writing itself; the pronunciation is therefore *pAleografía*, not *pàleografía*.

The other, less expected, pronunciation suggests a neologism, based on the model of *paleomarxista*, *paleocomunista*, *paleopositivista*, and so forth, implying perhaps an opposition to a corresponding form with *neo-*. The meaning conveyed is that of an old-style graphic designer; the word fits into the pattern of group 1 and has a secondary stress: *pàleográfico*, not *pAleográfico*.

There are words such as *telescopio*, *telefonia*, and so on, in which the last formative (*-scopio*, *-fonia*) is not an independent word. They belong to group 2 and are pronounced with secondary prominence (not secondary stress) on the first formative: *tElescópio*, *tElefonía*. The word *televisione* follows the same pattern, *-visione* functioning as a suffixoid rather than an independent word; *televisione*, in fact, means 'television,' or a 'television set,' not 'distant sight.' On the other hand, we have a series of compounds, such as *tèlespettatóre*, *tèleabbonáto*, *tèlegiornále*, with secondary stress and [ε] in the first syllable. They belong to group 1: the final formatives are independent words (*spettatore, abbonato, giornale*), and the first one (*tele-*) is a shortened form of *televisione*, rather than the Greek suffixoid *tele-*. *Teleabbonato* obviously means 'TV subscriber,' not 'distant subscriber.'

### 7.3. *Prefixes and Secondary Stress*

Comparable cases involve prefixes such as *pre-* and *ri-*. They may fit into group 1 and produce compounds with a final formative that is an independent word, in which case the prefix carries secondary stress; or they may fit into group 3 and produce derived forms, in which case the prefix does not carry secondary stress. In the former case the mechanism of word formation is synchronically productive and the grammatical analysis is transparent (*prèadamítico, prèindoeuropéo, prèfascísmo*, etc., *pre-* meaning 'before, of a previous period'); in the latter case the diachronic process and the morphological analysis may not be obvious (*preméssa, predicáto, pregiudicáto*, etc.).

It is easy to find minimal pairs, such as *pretensióne* 'pretension' vs *prètensióne* 'pre-tensioning' (a process in the building industry); *prefissáto* 'prefixed' vs *prèfissáto* 'fixed in advance'; *prelatíno* 'a little prelate' (diminutive of *prelato*) vs *prèlatíno* 'pre-Latin'; *riguárda* 'concerns' vs *rìguárda* 'looks again'; *rimacchiáre* 'to scribble poetry' vs *rìmacchiáre* 'to stain again.' One could add any number of examples with other prefixes or prefixoids, such as *atomístico* 'atomistic' (derived from *atomo*) vs *àtomístico* 'non Thomistic'; *tridentáto* 'provided with a trident' vs *trìdentáto* 'with three teeth'; *seminàto* 'participle of *seminare*' vs *sèminàto* 'half-born,' and so on.

According to Peperkamp, the examples with monosyllabic prefixes (such as those above) are homophonous, unless there is a contrastive accent.[34] For us, instead, as we have stated, these are minimal pairs, as lexical items, even though in fast, informal pronunciation the distinction may disappear – but this would equally affect many phonological oppositions that are obliterated in everyday performance. Comparable contrasts are accepted by Peperkamp for words with *ex-* (which she considers compounds), and for bisyllabic prefixes, for which she contrasts *s*[u:]*perveloce* (with a long [u:]) and *s*[u]*perstizioso* (with a short [u]); [ɛ]*uromissile* (with [ɛ], as the word is unfamiliar) and [e]*urosocialista* (with [e] as the word is in everyday use).[35]

As was argued above, the fact that individual examples are open to different interpretations should not cause surprise. This is a phenomenon that affects most aspects of language, not only prosodic ones, and makes an accurate recording of the data all the more useful and interesting.

NOTES

1 This chapter was originally prepared by A.L. Lepschy and me for a Danish Festschrift offered to Gunver Skytte: *L'infinito & oltre: Omaggio a Gunver Skytte*, ed. Hanne Jansen et al. (Odense: Odense University Press, 2002), 257–71. I am grateful to Vieri Samek-Lodovici and Helena Sanson for their comments on a previous version.

2 Giulio Lepschy, 'Il problema dell'accento latino,' *Annali della Scuola Normale Superiore di Pisa*, ser. 2, vol. 31 (1962), 199–246.

3 Giulio Lepschy, 'Note su accento e intonazione con riferimento all'italiano,' *Word* 24 (1968), 270–85 (also in G. Lepschy, *Saggi di linguistica italiana* [Bologna: il Mulino, 1978; 2nd ed. 1989], 111–26); Anna Laura Lepschy and Giulio Lepschy, *The Italian Language Today* (London: Hutchinson, 1977), 89–92, 152–5; Giulio Lepschy, 'Appunti sull'intonazione italiana,' *Annali della Scuola Normale Superiore di Pisa*, ser. 3, vol. 8:1 (1978), 275–92 (also in G. Lepschy, *Saggi di linguistica italiana*, 127–42).

4 Giulio Lepschy, 'Proposte per l'accento secondario,' *Italianist* 12 (1992), 117–28; also 'Altre note sull'accento secondario,' *Italianist* 13 (1993), 266–8.

5 Noam Chomsky, Morris Halle, and Fred Lukoff, 'On Accent and Juncture in

English,' in *For Roman Jakobson*, ed. Morris Halle et al. (The Hague: Mouton, 1956), 65–80.

6 Noam Chomsky and Morris Halle, *The Sound Pattern of English* (New York: Harper & Row, 1968).

7 Alan Prince and Paul Smolensky, *Optimality Theory: Constraint Interaction in Generative Grammar*, Rutgers Center for Cognitive Science Technical Report 2 (New Brunswick, N.J.: Rutgers University Press and Boulder: University of Colorado Press, 1993).

8 Bernard Bloch and George Leonard Trager, *Outline of Linguistic Analysis*, Special Publication of the Linguistic Society of America (Baltimore: Waverly Press, 1942), 47–8. The same symbols appear in George Leonard Trager and Henry Lee Smith Jr, *An Outline of English Structure*, Studies in Linguistics Occasional Papers, vol. 3, 3rd ed. (Washington, D.C.: American Council of Learned Societies, 1957; 1st ed., 1951), 35–7.

9 Frederick B. Agard and Robert J. Di Pietro, *The Sounds of English and Italian* (Chicago and London: University of Chicago Press, 1965).

10 N[ikolaj] S[ergeevich] Trubetzkoy, *Grundzüge der Phonologie*, Travaux du Cercle Linguistique de Prague, vol. 7, 2nd ed. (Göttingen: Vandenhoeck & Ruprecht, 1958; 1st ed., 1939); English trans. Christiane A.M. Baltaxe, Principles of Phonology (Berkeley and Los Angeles: University of California Press, 1969).

11 André Martinet, *Phonology as Functional Phonetics: Three Lectures Delivered before the University of London in 1946*, Publications of the Philological Society, vol. 15 (Oxford: Blackwell, 1949).

12 Chomsky, Halle, and Lukoff, 'On Accent and Juncture in English.'

13 Morris Halle, *The Sound Pattern of Russian* (The Hague: Mouton, 1959).

14 Erik Fudge, *English Word-Stress* (London: Allen & Unwin, 1984), 135.

15 Daniel Jones, *An English Pronouncing Dictionary (on Strictly Phonetic Principles)* (London: Dent, 1917; 2nd ed., 1924; 4th ed., 1937; 13th ed., 1967, ed. Alfred Charles Gimson).

16 Daniel Jones, *An English Pronouncing Dictionary*, 14th ed., ed. Alfred Charles Gimson, revision and supplement Susan Ramsaran (Cambridge: Cambridge University Press, 1991), xxiii.

17 Daniel Jones, *An English Pronouncing Dictionary*, 15th ed., ed. Peter Roach and James Hartman (Cambridge: Cambridge University Press, 1997).

18 John Christopher Wells, *Longman Pronunciation Dictionary* (Harlow, U.K.: Longman, 1990).

19  See, for example, Roger Kingdon, *The Groundwork of English Stress* (London: Longmans, Green, 1958); Chomsky and Halle, *Sound Pattern*; Fudge, *English Word-Stress*; Morris Halle and Jean-Roger Vergnaud, *An Essay on Stress* (Cambridge, Mass.: MIT Press, 1987); Luigi Burzio, *Principles of English Stress* (Cambridge: Cambridge University Press, 1994).

20  See, however, Amerindo Camilli, *Pronunzia e grafia dell'italiano* (Florence: Sansoni, 1941; 3rd ed. 1965); Giuseppe Malagoli, *L'accentazione italiana: Guida pratica* (Florence: Sansoni, 1946); G. Lepschy, 'Note su accento e intonazione con riferimento all'italiano,' 270–85; A.L. Lepschy and Giulio Lepschy, *Italian Language Today*, 89–92, 152–5; G. Lepschy, 'Appunti sull'intonazione italiana,' 275–92; G. Lepschy, 'Proposte,' 117–28; G. Lepschy, 'Altre note' 266–8; Pier Marco Bertinetto, 'L'accento secondario nella fonologia italiana. Analisi teorica e sperimentale,' in *Studi di fonetica e fonologia*, ed. Raffaele Simone et al., Pubblicazioni della Società di Linguistica italiana, vol. 9 (Rome: Bulzoni, 1976), 189–235; Pier Marco Bertinetto, *Strutture prosodiche dell'italiano* (Florence: Accademia della Crusca, 1981); Pier Marco Bertinetto, 'A proposito di alcuni recenti contributi alla prosodia dell'italiano,' *Annali della Scuola Normale Superiore di Pisa*, ser. 3, vol. 15, n. 2 (1985), 581–643; Irene Vogel and Sergio Scalise, 'Secondary Stress in Italian,' *Lingua* 58 (1982), 213–42; Willebrord Sluyters, 'Length and Stress Revisited: A Metrical Account of Diphthongization, Vowel Lengthening, Consonant Gemination and Word-Final Vowel Epenthesis in Modern Italian,' *Probus* 2:1 (1990), 65–102; Luigi Burzio and Elvira Di Fabio, 'Accentual Stability,' in *Issues and Theories in Romance Linguistics*, ed. Michael Lee Mazzola (Washington, D.C.: Georgetown University Press, 1994), 19–32; Haike Jacobs, 'How Optimal Is Italian Stress?' in *Linguistics in the Netherlands*, ed. Reineke Bok-Bennema and Crit Cremers, 11 (1994), 61–70; Maria Rosaria Caputo, 'Gradi accentuali nell'italiano parlato spontaneo,' *Studi italiani di linguistica teorica e applicata* 24:2 (1995), 421–7; Sharon Peperkamp, *Prosodic Words*, HIL Dissertations, vol. 34 (The Hague: Holland Institute of Generative Linguistics, 1997); Sharon Peperkamp, 'A Representational Analysis of Secondary Stress in Italian,' *Rivista di Linguistica* 9:1 (1997), 189–215.

21  Camilli, *Pronunzia*; Malagoli, *L'accentazione italiana*.

22  Vogel and Scalise, 'Secondary Stress in Italian.'

23  Bertinetto, 'L'accento secondario.'

24  G. Lepschy, 'Appunti sull'intonazione italiana.'

25  Vogel and Scalise, 'Secondary Stress in Italian.'

26 Peperkamp, 'A Representational Analysis.'

27 Tullio De Mauro, *Grande dizionario italiano dell'uso* (Turin: UTET, 1999).

28 G. Lepschy, 'Proposte'; G. Lepschy, 'Altre note.'

29 Bruno Migliorini, *Saggi sulla lingua del Novecento* (Florence: Sansoni, 1941; 3rd ed. 1963).

30 Chomsky and Halle, *Sound Pattern.*

31 Sergio Scalise, *Generative Morphology* (Dordrecht: Foris, 1984), 120; Sergio Scalise, *Morfologia* (Bologna: il Mulino, 1994), 136. See Peperkamp, *Prosodic Words*, 107.

32 Bertinetto, *Strutture prosodiche*; and 'A proposito di alcuni recenti contributi,' 637. Elsewhere, the Italian term 'contraccento' was used in this sense, see G. Lepschy, 'Proposte,' 121.

33 De Mauro, *Grande dizionario italiano dell'uso.*

34 Peperkamp, *Prosodic Words*, 71.

35 Ibid., 73–4, 144.

CHAPTER FIVE

# La Veniexiana: *A Venetian Play of the Renaissance*

In this chapter I shall discuss *La Veniexiana*, an anonymous play of
the first half of the sixteenth century, which I consider to be in
many ways the most striking play of the Italian Renaissance. I propose briefly to present (1) the manuscript and the history of its
publication; (2) the contents of the play; (3) the question of its
authorship and date; (4) the main features of the play: its structure
and theatrical qualities; (5) the two aspects that seem to me the
most interesting: the presentation of the female characters, and
their language; (6) finally, I shall analyse a detail of philological
interpretation in which questions of grammar and of critical perspective (a 'feminist' view of the play) interact and throw light on
each other.

## 1. *Manuscript and Editions*

*La Veniexiana* is preserved in a single manuscript in the Marciana
Library in Venice (MS. It. IX.288 [=6072]). The manuscript is of
the first half of the sixteenth century. It is bound together with
three other plays: *La Pastoral* by Beolco (or Ruzante, as he was
known, from the name of the protagonist of his plays)[1] and the
anonymous *La Bulesca*[2] and *Ardelia*.[3]

The four plays are transcribed by different hands. Beolco's *La Pastoral* originally belonged to MS. Marc. It. IX.71 (=5938), transcribed by Stefano Magno, who, according to Padoan, perhaps had
the idea of collecting together the four plays of MS. Marc. It.

IX.288.[4] At the end of the manuscript of *La Veniexiana* the copyist gives his name: Hieronymus Zarottus.[5] According to Padoan, this Girolamo Zarotto (i.e., Zarottus) was an actor specializing in female characters.[6]

*La Veniexiana* was first published by Emilio Lovarini (1928; Italian version, 1944 and 1947),[7] an erudite specialist of Pavana literature (see Gianfranco Folena's introduction to Lovarini's studies on Ruzante[8]). Subsequently, we have the editions (with introduction, facing Italian translation, and notes) by Ludovico Zorzi[9] and Giorgio Padoan.[10] The latter is significant for a new examination of the manuscript and for the scholarly apparatus; it is the basis for the new 'minor' edition, which presents some corrections and updatings.[11] The manuscript includes also poems by Navagero, Barignano, Fracastoro, Sannazaro, Verità, and Aretino, apparently to be sung as 'musical intermezzi'; they were inserted by Padoan into his 1994 edition: 'Canzone' by Andrea Navagero (p. 33); 'Madrigal' by Pietro Barignano (p. 37); 'Madrigal' by Girolamo Fracastoro (p. 67); 'Madrigal' by Jacopo Sannazaro (p. 75); 'Madrigal' by the Veronese Girolamo Verità (p. 89); 'Ballad' by Girolamo Fracastoro (p. 103); 'Ballad,' unpublished, attributed to P.A., presumably Piero Aretino (p. 115).

The play has been translated into various languages and repeatedly into English;[12] the main translations are listed in the bibliography of Padoan.[13] It has been frequently staged. I will recall the production by M. Scaparro in Rome (1984) and then in Los Angeles, in an adaptation and translation by Pier Maria Pasinetti, a staging that has been studied by Filippo Grazzini.[14] A film based on *La Veniexiana* (1985) was produced by Mauro Bolognini, filled with beautiful images but disappointing from other points of view and, unfortunately, spoken in Italian rather than in the original Venetian.

For the language of the play, a concordance, that is, a full lexical list, accompanied by some linguistic comments, has been published by Anna Laura Lepschy.[15] In the last section of this chapter I shall make use of her concordance and of an article written by us jointly.[16] When we were studying *La Veniexiana*, we consulted the manuscript at the Marciana library, and we can confirm that, for the relevant passages, the text we analyze is a faithful transcription of the manuscript. In general, however, the manuscript of *La Veniexiana* (in contrast with the three other plays with which it is bound) is practically indecipherable because the ink has almost completely faded. In effect, the pages look totally blank. Lovarini wrote about 'that unfortunate manuscript, where one can scarcely see the lines of writing, row upon row of bare willows shrouded in the winter mists' (quel disgraziato manoscritto, dove spesso si stenta a vedere le righe scritte, file di salici spogli, avvolti da nebbia invernale);[17] and Padoan,[18] who in general is rather harsh towards Lovarini and criticizes him for misusing chemical reagents, accepts that as early as 1928, when Lovarini first published the play, the manuscript 'was in a state of semi-illegibility' (versava in stato di quasi illeggibilità).[19]

## 2. *The Title*

The title probably means 'The Venetian Play,' rather than 'The Venetian Woman,'[20] as is the case with *La Cortigiana* by Aretino (rather than *La Piovana* and *Anconitata* by Ruzante, and *La Perugina* by Pennacchi). If it were 'The Woman from Venice,' it would probably refer to Valiera as the protagonist, rather than Anzola, notwithstanding the fascination the latter exerts on modern readers. The title, it should be pointed out, is unmistakably written with the letters '*ie*,' *Veniexiana*, and not *Venexiana*, in the original manuscript. Oddly, Lovarini had used *Venexiana* in his edition, and the form with the *-ie-* has become generally accepted only since Padoan's 1974 edition. The spelling *Veniexia, Veniexie* was common in early texts.

As far as the name of Venice is concerned, one may recall that traditionally *Venetia* was the name for the territory, and *Venetiae*, *Venezie* in the plural was the name for the city: Ruzante talks about the 'Segnoria de Venesia' (the territory), but in the *Parlamento* we find 'A' ghe son pur arivò a ste Veniesie!' (Here I am at last in these Veniesie). *Veneziano* was the adjective for Venice and the territory. *Veneto* is a more recent term, post-dating the fall of the Republic.[21] Contemporary dialectologists (e.g., Paola Benincà) use *Venetan* for 'of the Veneto,' and *Venetian* for 'of Venice.'[22]

### 3. *The Content of the Play*
The play has six characters: four Venetian women (two ladies, Valiera and Anzola, and their two servants, Oria and Nena, short for Elena); a Bergamask porter (Bernardo); and a young man from Lombardy (Iulio). Whereas the vernacular names are used in the exchanges in the play, the Latin forms (Valeria, Angela, Iulius, Bernardus) are found in the 'paratext' to indicate the characters. Iulio is a foreigner who is visiting Venice, in search of both amorous and financial success. He is fashionably dressed and coiffed, with a short velvet doublet: 'col vestio a la corta, de veluo' (I, 20); he is also described as dressed all in silk, very dashing: 'vestio de seda, tuto galante' (II, 36). His hair is black and plaited: 'cavei negri [...] trezolai' (I, 21–2; cf II, 36; II, 76). He is well spoken and very attractive to women.

Iulio has seen Valiera and wishes to try his luck with her. Valiera is attracted to him but plays hard to get.

Another lady, a young widow named Anzola, has also seen Iulio and finds him physically irresistible. She manages, with the help of her maid, Nena, and of Bernardo, the Bergamask porter who is related to Anzola's family, to get Iulio to visit her at home, where she makes love to him.

Valiera, who also accepts a date with Iulio, discovers his other tryst, is deeply offended, and dismisses him with harsh words. Finally, she swallows her pride, since she finds that she cannot resist her physical passion for the young man.

Iulio is a shallow character, who has little consideration for the two women he seduces and seems only concerned with his own pleasure and with the difficulties that may be caused by the pursuit of two women simultaneously.

### 4. *Author, Date, and Historical Background*

The manuscript gives the following: 'La Veniexiana. Comedia de [blank],' as if the author were known, but it had been decided to omit the name. Lovarini thought of Fracastoro as a possible author and of a date between 1509 and 1517, but without giving convincing reasons. The breakthrough was an article by Giorgio Padoan,[23] in which he stated that he had identified the two main female characters. Working in the Archive in Venice, he discovered that there were a Valiera Valier, who in 1535 had married Giacomo Semitecolo, 'avogador di comun,'[24] and also an Anzola Valier, widow of Marco Barbarigo, who died in 1535. Both women lived in the district of San Barnaba and the Toletta. Valiera had a sister Laura (see V, 58: 'la Laurina, mia suor'), who had married Mattio Barbarigo and was therefore the sister-in-law of Anzola. In I, 48, when Anzola complains that she has a high temperature, Nena suggests that they call 'misser Antonio, el nostro medico': there was, in fact, a well-known doctor from Crema, called Antonio Secco, who lived in the parish of San Barnaba.

The date suggested by Padoan for the play is 1536. The terminus post quem is the death of Francesco II Sforza on the night of 1 November 1535: only after this event could Bernardo have linked his 'fed gubelina' (Ghibelline beliefs) with Iulio: 'è la to, duchesche' (II, 104: it is yours, Dukely one). Bergamo had been conquered by Venice in 1427, annexed in 1430, and remained

Venetian until 1797. Milan, after the death of Francesco II passed under the rule of the emperor Charles V in 1535. The terminus ante quem is 1537, when carrying weapons was severely prohibited; after that date Iulio, who in the play goes around fully armed, would have been arrested immediately. In the play we find the following references to his bearing arms: 'Un forrestier vestio da sbisao, cun la spa' (I, 20: a foreigner dressed like a braggart, with a sword at his side); 'e adoprar questa persona e spada in suo servizio' (III, 49: and use this person and sword in her service); Anzola tells him: 'Spoia queste arme' (III, 52: Cast off these arms); Valiera observes: 'ha volesto venir armao' (IV, 17: he wanted to come armed), and Iulio replies: 'le arme son necessarie a un giovene' (IV, 18: arms are necessary to a young man).

The archival documents relating to the play are undoubtedly impressive. In fact, they seem almost too good to be true. On the other hand, the Venetian archives are so rich that it is not surprising that, if one looks hard enough, one can find anything one is looking for. At a conference held in London in April 1995 on 'The Jews of Italy,' I attended a fascinating lecture on Shakespeare's *Merchant of Venice* given by Brian Pullan, the eminent historian of Renaissance Venice, who reported that he had found documents showing that a warder of the Ghetto was called Gobbo and had a father called Gobbo – just as in Shakespeare.[25] Another example: in 1993 Claudio Povolo published *Il romanziere e l'archivista* (and in 1997, *L'intrigo dell'onore*) about a court case of 1605–7 at Orgiano in the Veneto, which had uncanny similarities to the story of Lucia and Don Rodrigo in Manzoni's *Promessi sposi*; it also transpired that in the 1820s, when Manzoni was writing his novel, the relevant file had gone missing while the archivist was a correspondent of Manzoni. Because the Austrian government did not allow archival documents to be freely consulted, they sometimes temporarily disappeared, as in this case.

Apparently, even an archivist would do anything in order to help a respected friend.[26]

If we return, with a slightly more confident attitude, to Padoan, we can rightly deduce that it would indeed have to be an extraordinary coincidence for the fictional characters of *La Veniexiana* to fit so well the data of the historical figures mentioned in the documents of the Venetian archive. Perhaps the words we read at the end of the manuscript, 'non fabula non comedia ma vera historia' (not a fable or a comedy but a true story), can, in fact, be taken at their face value rather than as a rhetorical flourish.

Padoan suggests that the play may have originated in the milieu of Giovan Francesco Valier, a patrician (albeit illegitimately born), a friend of Bembo, Bibbiena, Castiglione, Speroni, Aretino, and Ariosto, and author of risqué novellas about adulterous women. Ariosto mentions Valier in the *Orlando furioso* (27, 137–8; 46, 16). All his works were lost after he was hanged in 1542 for betraying secrets of state to a foreign power. The same conspiracy involved Costanza Fregoso, whose secretary Matteo Bandello wrote a novella (Parte IV, Nov. 26) in which we find the widow who entertains her lover at her home without revealing her own identity, a plot line also featured in a story by Masuccio Salernitano. The topic as such is obviously not particularly original. In any case, according to Padoan, Valier might have been not the author but perhaps the inspirer of the play.

## 5. *Main Features of the Play*

The author, as Padoan suggests, seems to be someone who was interested in the theatrical rather than the literary aspect of the work. In Italy, in the first part of the sixteenth century, we witness the birth (or perhaps the rebirth) of modern European theatre. There are some excellent studies on the subject. From an Italian perspective, I can mention the volume by Padoan,[27] and in English the book by Richard Andrews[28] and his chapter on sixteenth-century theatre in Brand and Pertile.[29] This is not the place to trace, even in the barest outline, the main trends of the Italian theatre of the time, from the discovery of Plautus, to Ariosto's *Cassaria* (1508) and *Suppositi* (1509), and on to powerful and original works, such as Machiavelli's *Mandragola* (1519), the incredibly authentic and ambivalent pavano (rustic Paduan) characters of Beolco (Ruzante), the polyglot experiments of Calmo in the *Rodiana* (1541), and the genius of Giordano Bruno's *Candelaio* (1582).

Even in the context of such a complex and rich background, the *Veniexiana* stands out as a truly exceptional, and in many ways unique and unclassifiable, play. So exceptional, in fact, that in some of the standard presentations of sixteenth-century theatre it is not mentioned at all[30] or is set aside as something that requires a separate discussion.[31] Yet the value of the play was acknowledged from the start by its editors, Lovarini,[32] then Padoan, who writes about the 'unique and extraordinary quality' (singolarità e straordinarietà) of the *Veniexiana*,[33] and contemporary critics, such as Emilio Pasquini, who calls it 'one of the major comedies of the sixteenth century,' and Siro Ferrone, who considers it 'a true theatrical masterpiece' (un vero e proprio capolavoro drammaturgico).[34]

The manuscript marks the division into five acts, on the model of classical plays. According to Andrews,[35] this subdivision was imposed by scholars in late antiquity; but obviously, we must remember Horace's precept in *Ars Poetica* (189–90): 'a play that aspires to be demanded and demanded again, need not be shorter, nor longer than the fifth act' (neve minor neu sit quinto productior actu / fabula, quae posci vult et spectanda reposci). In a sense, the play can be said to respect the unities of time, space and action. Padoan notes that 'the achievement of the prescribed unities is laborious' (laborioso il conseguimento delle prescritte unità), since the changes of scene are sudden and the chronological breaks are marked, but the action is uninterrupted throughout the four days and three nights of amorous encounters.[36] The original of Aristotle's *Poetics* was published in 1536, but of course, one may respect the Aristotelian unities without having read Aristotle. A fine critic such as Diego Valeri comments on the play as follows:

> composed without any regard for pseudo-Aristotelian dogmas, it consists of a free sequence of episodes, some short, some long, with very frequent changes of scene, so that from a technical point of view it could seem an extraordinary anticipation of plays by Shakespeare and Musset, were it not that the subject matter is simple in the extreme and the art genuinely realistic (Condotta senza nessun riguardo dei dogmi pseudo-aristotelici, essa consiste in una libera successione di episodi, brevi e lunghi, con frequentissimi mutamenti di scena; di modo che potrebbe apparire, nel rispetto tecnico, una stupefacente anticipazione della commedia di Shakespeare e di Musset. Senonché il soggetto è semplice all'estremo, e l'arte schiettamente realistica).[37]

The acts are subdivided into scenes: three in Act I, five in Act II, two in Act III, five in Act IV, and three in Act V. The division into scenes seems to have been introduced by Padoan on the basis of criteria that are not immediately clear: usually, but not always, a change of scene corresponds to a change in the locality or in the participants in the dialogue. In Padoan's edition there are eighteen scenes overall, nine taking place in the street, five in Valiera's home, and four in Anzola's home.

The action covers four days:

First day, in Act I: afternoon in the street and in Valiera's room; night-time in Nena's bedroom.

Second day, in Act II: morning and afternoon, in the street and in

Anzola's bedroom; Act III: night-time, in Valiera's home, and in Anzola's home, various rooms.

Third day, in Act IV, scenes 1 to 4: morning and afternoon in the street; night-time in Valiera's home and in the street.

Fourth day, in Act IV, scene 5, and in Act V: morning in the street, evening in the street and in Valiera's home.

The development of the action is straightforward, with Iulio seducing, or rather being seduced, first by Anzola (Act III, scene 2), with Nena and Bernardo acting as helpers; and then by Valiera (Act V, scene 3), with Oria acting as helper. More than by the structural organization of the scenic action, taking place in a complex patterning of outside vs inside (the street vs the home), and on higher and lower levels (rooms upstairs vs downstairs), one is struck by the theatrical quality of the exchanges and how they seem to suggest gestures and movement, with a rare balance between the written text (which usually predominates in literary plays) and the physicality of the action in the popular and commedia dell'arte tradition.

### 6. *The Female Characters and Their Language*

The two aspects that to me seem most striking and make *La Veniexiana* unique in the whole of sixteenth-century theatre are the language and the representation of female characters.

For the language of the play, there is, of course, a tradition of multilingualism in Venetian culture; Latin and literary Italian are used at a high level, Venetian being the ordinary medium of communication, and also are employed in different registers, from the high level of the law-courts and the administration, to the lower levels of the fishermen and the 'arsenalotti,' the workers of the Arsenale or shipbuilding yards. Between Venetian and Italian an intermediate area was occupied by the 'cancelleresco' language, that is, the chancery idiom used in texts such as the *Diari* by Marin Sanudo, the extended day-to-day account of private and public events in Venice during the first part of the Cinquecento.[38] In addition, a varied tapestry of 'foreign' languages could be heard in Venice, from diplomats, travellers, pilgrims, and merchants, in their fonteghi[39] and commercial centres, where most of the western European languages, as well as Arabic, Turkish, Greek (and the Greghesco[40] of the Stradioti), and Slavic (with a rich production of Schiavonesca literature) were spoken. There was the speech of socially characterized figures, such as the Bergamask of porters or Zanni, and the *pavano* of the peasants. Around the Ghetto the Yiddish of the Ashkenazi Jews mingled with the Ladino of the Sephardic Jews (as well as the Turkish and Arabic of Middle Eastern Jews).

Polyglot plays reached a virtuoso peak with Giancarli's *Zingana*, and Calmo's *Rodiana*, in which Neapolitan, French, Raguseo, Spanish, Florentine, Pugliese, Mantuan, Genoese, and Arabic were used. Critics usually point out two distinct elements in these feats of multilingualism, one being documentary realism, the other comic effect.[41]

What we find in the *Veniexiana* is quite different. Of the languages of the play, the Italian of Iulio and the Bergamask of Bernardo are the odd men out. They are not used for comic characterization, and they allow the individual psychological features of the characters to emerge: shallow, self-centred, and superficially hedonist in the case of Iulio (his Italian being artificial and slightly stilted, not adhering to the polished, sophisticated standards set in Bembo's prose); and rougher, down-to-earth, full of expressions linked to bodily functions, direct and forthright in the case of Bernardo (his Bergamask corresponding to an image of 'uncouthness,' which has deep roots, with a long tradition of poems *alla bergamasca*).

What represents 'normality,' what appears to be the 'unmarked' choice (against which both Iulio's Italian and Bernardo's Berga-mask stand out as 'marked'), is the Venetian of the four women. The impression is that what we have here is a 'language,' not a 'dia-lect,' as Folena notes, in a penetrating passage about Goldoni's Venetian: it was a fully grown 'lenguazo.'[42] The language used by the four women of *La Veniexiana* is not subordinated to a 'higher' standard; it does not suggest a 'diglossic' situation (and even less does it appear to be a low variety in a diglossic community). It is an idiom used with full confidence by the two ladies and the two maids, who are able to exploit all the appropriate keys and regis-ters. However illusory the sensation may be that a written work appropriately reproduces a real-life dialogue, it is impossible to avoid the feeling that we are being offered a text that reflects speech perhaps better than any other in Italian literature, with a grace, a spontaneity, and an immediacy that one normally expects only from spoken language.[43]

The second aspect I mentioned concerns not only the surpris-ingly effective presentation of spoken language in the play, but also the fact that the female viewpoint is conveyed by the four women, a female perspective represented in a manner that is, as far as I know, unique in Italian premodern literature. Particularly surpris-ing and unexpected is the fact that we have two women who vie with each other for the possession of one man. The two women are active and take the initiative, while Iulio is a passive target of desire. He is treated as a sexual object, and the two women compete to conquer him. Thus, the standard pattern, in which there are two or more men competing for the favours of one woman, is turned upside down.

Anzola and Valiera (to the accompaniment of basically sympa-thetic, if occasionally plaintive comments from their maids) reveal their sexual desire for the young foreigner and their wish to take their pleasure of him, with an astonishing frankness. The sensuality is particularly explicit in the more mature of the two, Anzola, who is a widow. According to Attilio Momigliano, 'Anzola's sensual cravings are transfigured by such a power of passion and poetry' that the third scene of Act I 'is a masterpiece which is not surpassed by the most famous scenes of the erotic theatre of any period.'[44] Diego Valeri makes some fine observations on the 'tone of melancholy which lingers, now more lightly, now more heavily, on the intoxicated words of the two women in love. Their love is uneasy, restless, troubled: conscious one would say, of its fleetingness ... There is a certain delicacy, a certain nobility in the sentiments of the two women *folles de leurs corps*; there is the melancholy of sensuality' (un accento di malinconia che si posa, or lieve or grave, sulle parole ebbre delle due innamorate. L'amor loro è inquieto, agitato, quasi affannoso: conscio, si direbbe, della propria caducità ... C'è, insomma, una certa gentilezza, una certa nobiltà, nel sentire delle due donne *folles de leurs corps*; c'è la malinconia della sensualità).[45]

Anzola goes to Nena's bedroom and tells her that she is on fire and needs the young man she has seen. The dialogue continues as follows (the English translation by C.F. Balducci is added in brackets):

NENA: Iiih! El xè quel bel fio? Che voleu far d'un puto? [Eeee! That handsome young guy? What would you do with a boy?]

ANGELA: Che, an? Varda sta bestia! Ti no scià, no? [What, eh? Look, you beast! As if you didn't know?]

NENA: Disé un puoco zò che volé far. [Tell me what you'd do.]

ANGELA: Butarghe cusì le braze al collo, zicar, quelle lavrine, e tegnirlo streto streto. [Throw my arms around him, like this, suck his lips and hold on, oh so tight!]

NENA: E po' no altro? [And then nothing else?]

ANGELA: La lenguina in boca. [The tongue in my mouth.]

NENA: Meio lo saverae far mi cha esso. [I'd know how to do that better than he would!]

ANGELA: Quella bochina dolçe tegnerla per mi, cussì, sempre sempre! [That sweet little mouth, all mine, forever and ever!]

NENA: Sté indrio ché me sofoghé! [Go away, you're smothering me!]

ANGELA: Caro, dolçe pì che no xè el zùcaro! [Dearest, sweetheart, sweeter even than sugar.]

NENA: Vu no v'arecordé che sun donna. [You're forgetting I'm a woman.]

ANGELA: Sun morta, mi. Sudo in aqua, tuta. [And I'm dying. Sweating, wet every place.]

NENA: Gran merçé! perché vu fe matiere. [Mercy! You're acting crazy.]

ANGELA: Passarà pur la note, e vegnerà doman. [This night will pass. Tomorrow will come.]

NENA: Che, doman? Disé: che fareu doman? [What, tomorrow? Say it: what will you do tomorrow?]

ANGELA: Voio aver quel fio, mi. [I want that boy!]

NENA: A che modo voleu far? [How do you plan to get him?]

ANGELA: Cun denari e cun presenti. [With money and presents.]

NENA: Sì, cun zente che 'l sappa menar. [Yes, with people who know how to arrange it.]

ANGELA: Cun tuto ziò che ti dirà. [With everything I've got, you might say (i.e., with everything that you will say).]

NENA: Orsù, torné al vostro luogo, e dormé. [In that case, better go back to your room and go to sleep.]

ANGELA: Voio star qua. E, se ti vul che dorma, gèttame cussì le to braze; e mi sererò gli ochii, e te crederò el fio. [I'd rather stay here. And, if you want me to sleep, grab me, like so, in your arms; and I'll shut my eyes and pretend you are that boy.]

NENA: Voleu cusì? [Like it like this?]

ANGELA: Sì, cara fia. [Yes, dear girl.]

NENA: Me credeu, mo? [Believe that I'm him, now?]

ANGELA: No ancora: de qua un pezeto. [Not yet: in a little while.]

NENA: Vogio dormir, mi. Guardé: non me strenzé. [I'd like to get some sleep. Watch it: quit hugging me!]

ANGELA: Vostu farme un piaser? [Do me a favor?]

NENA: Che? [What?]

ANGELA: Cara, dolçe, sta' cusì un puoco; e po' comenza a biastemar, azò che ti creda omo. [Dear, Sweetheart, keep this up a little longer; then start to talk dirty, so I'll be convinced you are a man.]

NENA: No sciò zò che dir, mi. [I don't know what to say, not me!]

ANGELA: Biastema el corpo de Cristo, menzona le parolle sporche: co' fa i omeni. [Curse the Body of Christ, use dirty words, the way men do.]

NENA: Disé: che parolle? [Tell me, what words?]

ANGELA: Quelle sporcarie che se dise in bordello, no sastu? [Those piggish things they say in whorehouses, don't you know any?]

NENA: Se no dormo, le dirò; ma se dormo, non dirò gnente, mi. [If I don't sleep, I shall say them; but if I fall asleep, I won't say anything.]

ANGELA: Cara Nena, fa' un puoco el sbisao, per mio amor. [Nena, dear, just for a while, play the man, for my love's sake.][46]

## 7. *Feminism and Philology*

I should like to analyse a few passages for which the perspective I have highlighted seems to be relevant.

Consider the last sentence of the Prologue: 'E non ve imaginate altrimenti donne, se non quanto lo vederete, vestite: che poi, spoliate, siano non amate, ma amanti, insieme cun voi.'[47] (The interpretation is controversial, as is made clear in the discussion that follows.) For 'amate' the manuscript gives 'amãte' (i.e. 'amante') which has been emended by Lovarini into 'amande' and by Padoan into 'amate.' The contrast between being 'loved' and 'loving' was common at the time. Padoan recalls obvious texts, such as Bembo's *Asolani* and Equicola's *Natura de amore*, and men-

tions a passage in Sperone Speroni's *Dialogo di amore* in which
Nicolò Grazia observes: 'I know not a few women who love
greatly, but the same ones are also loved, in such a way that rather
than lovers (*amanti*) they should be called loved ones (*amate*)' (Io
conosco non poche donne, le quali amano grandemente, ma quelle
istesse sono anche amate in maniera, che più tosto amate che
amanti dovrebbono essere nominate); and later: 'man loves more
passionately his lady, than she loves him [...] for which deservedly
we shall call them [the women] loved ones (*amate*), and ourselves
[the men] lovers (*amanti*)' (l'uomo ama più fieramente la donna
sua, che ella non ama lui [...] per la qual cosa meritamente loro
amate, e noi amanti nominaremo).[48] According to Padoan, the
prologue of *La Veniexiana* at this point opposes the prevailing fashion of Petrarchist idealization. There is a traditional interpretation
going back to Lovarini (and still preferred by some scholars, such
as Zorzi, and Giovanni Aquilecchia),[49] which refers to male actors,
dressed as women, playing the roles of female characters. Inciden-
tally, exactly when women started appearing on stage seems not to
be known with certainty. All the critics I have read who have com-
mented on this point concerning *La Veniexiana* state that it is out
of the question that the play (if it was ever staged at the time) had
female actors.[50]

Lovarini notes that 'the prologue warns the viewers that they
should imagine that those are women only because they see them
dressed as women; but once they are undressed, they will turn out
to be not "amande," that is, to be loved, but "amanti," i.e., (active)
lovers, like the viewers, i.e., males' (il prologhista ammonisce gli
spettatori che non si figurino esser donne quelle se non perché le
vedono così vestite, le quali spogliate non sono poi *amande*, cioè da
amarsi, ma *amanti* come loro, cioè maschi).[51] Padoan instead trans-
lates: 'Do not imagine women as being different from you, other
than in as far as you can see it when they are dressed: when they are

undressed (you should imagine) that they are not loved ones [amate], but active subjects of love in their own right, just as you are' (E non immaginatevi diverse da voi le donne, se non per quanto lo vedrete, quando sono vestite: le quali poi, spogliate, siano non amate, ma esse stesse soggetti attivi d'amore, come voi siete).[52]

Padoan believes that Lovarini later changed his mind, and in his editions of 1944 and 1947 proposed a reading that referred to women as active lovers rather than to male actors playing the parts of female characters. According to Larivaille, the Prologue invites the audience not to undress women in their minds, considering them as their lovers, but only to imagine them as beings to be loved ('amande') intellectually, fully dressed, as they are seen on the stage.[53] This invitation is linked to the previous sentence, in which the audience is exhorted to approach love 'with the intellect and not with the sense[s]' ('co l'intelletto e non col senso'). The Prologue would then be offering a moralistic warning against the sensuality that triumphs in the play. For Padoan, the Prologue is saying: do not imagine that women are different from you, just because you see them dressed differently. Once you remove the dress and they are free from the conventions imposed by society, you would see that women, too, just like you men, are active subjects of love, not objects. This interpretation may be strengthened by another passage, if we accept the controversial, but stimulating reading Carlo Dionisotti suggests.

I would like to introduce a personal element here. As I mentioned, my wife, Anna Laura Lepschy, published in 1996 a concordance of *La Veniexiana*. On receiving a copy, Dionisotti, as was his wont, sent her an interesting letter with comments and observations. One note was particularly striking. He had identified two verb forms (*ti tocasse* and *ti tochi*), which the concordance recorded as second-person singular, with a subject pronoun ('you touched' and 'you touch'). He thought these forms were, instead, third-person singular, with object pronouns. Let us look at the passages. During the erotic scene between Anzola and Iulio, in Act III, scene 2, Anzola states that she cannot bear the idea of Iulio making love to another woman:

> Aldi zò che ti digo: se me credesse che ti tocasse altra donna, moreria qua d'angonissa in le to braze (III, 108).
>
> (A: Listen to what I am telling you: if I were to think that you were to touch another woman, I would die of torment here in your arms;
> B: Listen to what I am telling you: if I were to think that another woman were to touch you, I would die of torment here in your arms).

Later she gives him a jewel:

> perché ti sappa che l'amor mio xè che no ti tochi altra donna che viva (III, 144)
>
> (A: so that you know that my love is [such] that you must touch no other woman alive;
> B: so that you know that my love is [such] that no other woman alive must touch you).

Interpretation A is the one given by all the editors and translators that I have consulted. It seems that they have not even considered the possibility of another reading. Dionisotti, however, comments in his letter as follows, upholding interpretation B:

> The question of *La Veniexiana* is not simple. Because in that play the person *who touches*, the person who proposes and initiates love is the woman, and the rivalry is between two women over one man, and each of the two sniffs her rival from afar and fears her. I think therefore that in these two parallel passages (*che ti tocasse altra donna* and *che no ti tochi*

*altra donna*) *ti* is the object, not the subject. I can understand that, trusting the traditional rule of the male touch, Lovarini gave a different interpretation. Nor am I surprised by Padoan.

(La questione della Veneziana non è semplice. Perché in quella commedia *chi tocca*, chi propone e inizia l'amore è la donna, e la rivalità è di due donne per un uomo, e ciascuna delle due fiuta a distanza e teme la rivale. Pertanto credo che nei due passi paralleli (che ti tocasse altra donna e che no ti tochi altra donna) *ti* sia oggetto, non soggetto. Mi spiego che, fidando nella regola tradizionale del tocco maschile, Lovarini abbia interpretato altrimenti. Né mi stupisco di Padoan.)

At first sight, a reader familiar with modern Venetian may feel that Dionisotti is looking at the text with, so to speak, Italian rather than Venetian eyes and that the interpretation of dialect speakers such as Lovarini, Zorzi, and Padoan is obviously correct. Reading a sixteenth-century text on the basis of twentieth-century grammar, however, is obviously not a method to be recommended. If we look at the language of the *Veniexiana* rather than at the modern dialect, the solution is not as simple as it seemed at the beginning.

We have to face three grammatical questions, concerning (a) the form of the pronoun, (b) the morphology of the verb, and (c) the position of the negative particle.

(a) In modern Venetian, *ti* is the form of the second-person subject and *te* of the object: interpretation B would therefore require *te*. Yet in the Venetian of the four women, I have found for the direct object twelve cases of *te* and seven of *ti*; and for the indirect object seven cases of *te* and fourteen of *ti*. Overall, the second-person object pronoun, direct and indirect, appears nineteen times as *te*, and twenty-one as *ti*. One could analyze the individual examples, looking for possible Italian influences, but this would not take us very far. One simply has to accept that the object interpretation of *ti*, required by reading B, is richly documented and well within the boundaries of the *usus scribendi* of the *Veniexiana*. In fact, object *ti* (twenty-one occurrences) slightly prevails over *te* (nineteen occurrences).

(b) In interpretation B, with object *ti* and *altra donna* as subject, *tocasse* corresponds to the modern Venetian form, but for *tochi* one would expect *toca*. Conversely, in interpretation A, with subject *ti* and *altra donna* as object, for *tocasse* one would expect *tocassi* in modern Venetian, while *tochi* would be unchanged. Here, too, one finds in the *Veniexiana* a second-person imperfect subjunctive in *-e* (side by side with *-i*), and cases of third-person present subjunctive in *-i* (side by side with *-a*). Again, interpretation B (which seems more feasible than the traditional one for *tocasse* and less so for *tochi*) is in both cases compatible with the usage of the play.

(c) The position of the negative particle is relevant for the second example (§144): 'che no ti tochi altra donna.' Here, interpretation B, with the negative to the left of the object, causes no difficulties. It is interpretation A, with the negative to the left of the subject pronoun, as in modern Venetian, that is problematic. In Old Venetian the negative particle appears on the right of the subject pronoun (for instance, *s'el non fose*, 'if he were not,' instead of the modern Venetian *se no'l fuse*). In *La Veniexiana* usage oscillates, with a preference for the modern order in the third person (cases like *no la puol*, 'she can't' (II, 12) prevail over those like *la non die*, 'she must not' (IV, 48)); and a preference for the old order in the second-person (cases like *ti no vegnarè*, 'you'll not come' (III, 116) prevail over those like *se no ti mi dà*, 'if you don't give me' (III, 85)). Therefore, interpretation A of *che no ti tochi*, with subject *ti*, seems possible, but is less consistent with the usage of *La Veniexiana* than reading B.[54]

To sum up, concerning who is touching whom in these two passages of *La Veniexiana*, it seems to me that grammatically both choices are open, but Dionisotti's preference for the female touch is both more unexpected and more consistent with the whole orientation of the play, in which women do take the initiative and are active sexual subjects rather than passive objects. Whether this interpretation makes *La Veniexiana* a 'feminist' play (whatever the term 'feminist' may mean with reference to early sixteenth-century Venetian culture) is more problematic. One of my students once asked me whether anyone had considered the possibility that the author was a woman. Not as far as I know, was my answer. In fact, it seems to me that the text is also open to a male-oriented interpretation. It seems that actors and audience were exclusively male, and men's contemplation of females' being forward, active initiators in sexual matters is traditionally considered enjoyable: what feminists would call the patriarchal, male chauvinist gaze.[55]

In Ruzante the peasant is laughed at by his urban, upper-class audience, and at the same time he challenges in a transgressive and disturbing manner the audience's conventional assumptions. In a similar fashion we could say that the ambivalence of the message in *La Veniexiana* adds to the power of this exceptional text.

NOTES

1  Angelo Beolco il Ruzante, *La pastoral. La prima oratione. Una lettera giocosa. Testo critico, tradotto ed annotato*, ed. Giorgio Padoan, Medioevo e umanesimo, vol. 32 (Padua: Antenore, 1978).
2  Bianca Maria Da Rif, *La letteratura 'alla bulesca.' Testi rinascimentali veneti* (Padua: Antenore, 1984).

3  Anonimo veneziano del '500, *Ardelia. Commedia. Testo critico, introduzione, glossario e note*, ed. Franca Carnasciali (Florence: Il Fauno editore, 1982); *La commedia* Ardelia. *Edizione, introduzione e commento*, ed. Annalisa Agrati, Biblioteca degli Studi mediolatini e volgari, new ser., vol. 13 (Pisa: Pacini, 1994).

4  Beolco il Ruzante, *La pastoral*.

5  Originally transcribed as Zarellus or Zanettus by Emilio Lovarini in his 1928 edition, and Giorgio Padoan in his 1974 edition (see below, n. 7 and 10, respectively).

6  See Giorgio Padoan in his 1994 edition (see below, n. 11), 11.

7  Emilio Lovarini, ed., *La Venexiana. Commedia di ignoto cinquecentista*, Nuova scelta di curiosità letterarie inedite o rare, vol. 1 (Bologna: Zanichelli, 1928); *La Venexiana: Commedia in cinque atti. Riduzione italiana e presentazione di Emilio Lovarini, Teatro*. Raccolta di commedie di ogni epoca. ser. 1, vol. 11 (Turin: Edizioni di Il Dramma. Società Editrice Torinese, 1944); also *La Venexiana. Commedia*, Collezione in ventiquattresimo (Florence: Le Monnier, 1947).

8  Emilio Lovarini, *Studi sul Ruzante e la letteratura pavana*, ed. Gianfranco Folena (Padua: Antenore, 1965), vii–lxxix.

9  Ludovico Zorzi, ed., Ignoto veneto del Cinquecento, *La Venexiana*, Collezione di teatro, vol. 63 (Turin: Einaudi, 1965).

10  *La Veniexiana: Commedia di anonimo veneziano del Cinquecento*, trans. and ann. Giorgio Padoan, Medioevo e Umanesimo, vol. 20 (Padua: Antenore, 1974).

11  *La Veniexiana*, ed. Giorgio Padoan, with facing Italian version, Letteratura universale Marsilio. Esperia (Venice: Marsilio, 1994).

12  Matilde Valenti Pfeiffer, ed., *La Venexiana: A Sixteenth Century Venetian Comedy*, with introduction and English translation (New York: S.F. Vanni, 1950).

13  Padoan, *La Veniexiana*, 1994.

14  Filippo Grazzini, 'Amor di donne e amor di città: la totalità erotica della *Veniexiana*,' in *Forma e parola: Studi in memoria di Fredi Chiappelli*, ed. Dennis J. Dutschke et al. (Rome: Bulzoni, 1992), 305–26.

15  Anna Laura Lepschy, *Varietà linguistiche e pluralità di codici nel Rinascimento*, Saggi di 'Lettere Italiane,' vol. 51 (Florence: Olschki, 1996). See also Günter Holtus, 'La *Veniexiana* fonte di strutture e di elementi del parlato,' in *Linguistica e dialettologia veneta: Studi offerti a Manlio Cortelazzo dai colleghi stranieri*, ed. Günter Holtus and Michael Metzeltin (Tübingen: Narr, 1983), 55–70.

16 Anna Laura Lepschy and Giulio Lepschy, 'La *Veniexiana* e il tocco femminile.' To appear in the Festschrift for Christian Bec, *Florence-Venice: Des origines au XXe siècle.*

17 Lovarini, *La Venexiana*, 1947.

18 Padoan, *La Venexiana*, 1974, 40.

19 Padoan, *La Venexiana*, 1994, 21.

20 Padoan, *La Venexiana*, 1994, 11, 124.

21 Gianfranco Folena, *Scrittori e scritture: Le occasioni della critica* (Bologna: il Mulino, 1997), 324.

22 See Martin Maiden and Mair Parry, eds, *The Dialects of Italy* (London and New York: Routledge, 1997); Glanville Price, ed., *Encyclopedia of the Languages of Europe* (Oxford: Blackwell, 1998).

23 Giorgio Padoan, 'La "Veniexiana": "non fabula non comedia ma vera historia,"' *Lettere italiane* 19 (1967), 1–54.

24 An important magistrate (a kind of state attorney or attorney-general), whose function was to make sure that the laws were correctly applied by the organs of the Republic. See Giovanni Scarabello and Paolo Morachiello, *Guida alla civiltà di Venezia* (Milan: Mondadori, 1987) 15, 228.

25 Brian Pullan, 'Shakespeare's Shylock: Evidence from Venice,' in *The Jews of Italy: Memory and Identity*, ed. Barbara Garvin and Bernard Cooperman, Studies and Texts in Jewish History and Culture (Bethesda, Md.: University Press of Maryland, 2000), 193–208.

26 Claudio Povolo, *Il romanziere e l'archivista, da un processo veneziano del '600 all'anonimo manoscritto dei Promessi sposi* (Venice: Istituto Veneto, 1993); Claudio Povolo, *Un intrigo dell'onore: Poteri e istituzioni nella Repubblica di Venezia tra Cinquecento e Seicento* (Verona: Cierre Edizioni, 1997).

27 Giorgio Padoan, *L'avventura della commedia rinascimentale* (Padua: Piccin Nuova Libraria & Vallardi, 1996).

28 Richard Andrews, *Scripts and Scenarios: The Performance of Comedy in Renaissance Italy* (Cambridge: Cambridge University Press, 1993).

29 Richard Andrews, 'Theatre,' in *The Cambridge History of Italian Literature*, ed. Peter Brand and Lino Pertile (Cambridge: Cambridge University Press, 1996), 277–98.

30 Ibid.

31 Andrews, *Scripts and Scenarios*, 144.

32 Lovarini, *La Venexiana*, 1928; see also Alfred Mortier, 'Une comédie vénitienne de la Renaissance,' *Études Italiennes*, new ser., vol. 2:4 (1932), 265–75;

Bodo L.O. Richter, 'La *Venexiana* in the Light of Recent Criticism,' in *The Drama of the Renaissance: Essays for Leicester Bradner*, ed. Elmer M. Blistein (Providence, R.I.: Brown University Press, 1970). Andrews offers a penetrating discussion of this play in 'Staging *La Veniexiana* or How to Ruin a Perfectly Good Script,' in *Scenery, Set and Staging in the Italian Renaissance: Studies in the Practice of Theatre*, ed. Christopher Cairns (Lampeter: Edwin Mellen Press, 1996), 101–19.

33 Padoan, *La Venexiana di Anonimo del Cinquecento*, adattamento di Giorgio Padoan, Collana del Teatro di Roma 20 (Rome: Officina Edizioni, 1984), 7.

34 In Enrico Malato, *Storia della letteratura italiana*, vol. 3, *Il Quattrocento* (Rome: Salerno Editrice, 1996), 875, 953–4.

35 Andrews, 'Theatre,' 278.

36 Padoan, *La Veniexiana*, 1994, 10.

37 Diego Valeri, 'Caratteri e valori del teatro comico,' in *La civiltà veneziana del Rinascimento* (Florence: Sansoni, 1958, 11); originally published 1949.

38 A.L. Lepschy, *Varietà*, 33–51.

39 This is the traditional Venetian term for warehouse: in Italian 'fondaco.'

40 Venetian form for Greek (also 'grechesco').

41 Manlio Cortelazzo, 'Esperienze ed esperimenti plurilinguistici,' in *Storia della cultura veneta*, vol. 3:2 (Vicenza: Neri Pozza, 1980), 183–213; see also Ivano Paccagnella, *Il fasto delle lingue: plurilinguismo letterario nel Cinquecento* (Rome: Bulzoni, 1984); Gianfranco Folena, *Il linguaggio del caos: Studi sul plurilinguismo rinascimentale* (Turin: Bollati Boringhieri, 1991).

42 Gianfranco Folena, *L'italiano in Europa: Esperienze linguistiche del Settecento* (Turin: Einaudi 1983), 91–2.

43 For some considerations of the way in which the four women speak see A.L. Lepschy, *Varietà*, 53–68.

44 Attilio Momigliano, *Storia della letteratura italiana*, vol. 1, *Dalle origini al Tasso* (Messina-Milan: Principato, 1933), 266–7.

45 Valeri, 'Caratteri e valori del teatro comico,' 15–16.

46 Padoan, *La Veniexiana*, 1994, 41–3, §62–95; *La Veniexiana (1535)*, trans. Carolyn Feleppa Balducci, with introduction and notes by M.W. Walsh, Carleton Renaissance Plays in Translation, vol. 34 (Ottawa: Dovehouse Editions, 2000), 39–40.

47 Padoan, *La Veniexiana*, 1994, 27, §7.

48 Sperone Speroni, *Opere*, Tome 2, vol. 1 (Venice: D. Occhi, 1740), 32–3.

49 Zorzi, *La Venexiana*, 10; Aquilecchia, personal communication.

50 Andrews, 'Staging *La Veniexiana*,' 107–8, observes: 'We cannot put a secure date on the first appearance of a professional female actor before a respectable Italian public – the first one of which I know is 1548, in Lyons'; see also 114.

51 Lovarini, *La Venexiana*, 1928, 20.

52 Padoan, *La Veniexiana*, 1974, 70; and *La Veniexiana*, 1994, 26.

53 Paul Larivaille, 'La *Veniexiana* ou les ressources du langage honnête: Censure et théâtre à Venise,' in *Le pouvoir et la plume: Incitation, contrôle et répression dans l'Italie du XVIᵉ siècle. Actes du colloque* ... Aix-en-Provence, Marseille, 14–16 mai 1981. Centre International de Recherche sur la Renaissance Italienne, vol. 10 (Paris: Université de la Sorbonne Nouvelle, 1982), 172.

54 See discussion in A.L. Lepschy and G. Lepschy, 'La *Veniexiana* e il tocco femminile,' and relevant examples in Alfredo Stussi, *Testi veneziani del Duecento e dei primi del Trecento*, Studi di lettere, storia e filosofia pubblicati dalla Scuola Normale Superiore di Pisa, vol. 34 (Pisa: Nistri Lischi, 1965); Marco Polo, *Il 'Milione' veneto, ms CM 211 della Biblioteca Civica di Padova*, ed. Alvaro Barbieri and Alvise Andreose (Venice: Marsilio, 1999); Andrea Berengo, *Lettres d'un marchand vénitien: Andrea Berengo (1553–1556)*, ed. Ugo Tucci, École Pratique des Hautes Études, VIe section, Affaires et gens d'affaires, vol. 10 (Paris: SEVPEN, 1957).

55 See interesting observations on this question in Andrews, 'Staging *La Veniexiana*,' 114–18.

# CHAPTER SIX

# Carlo Dionisotti, 1908–1998: A Memoir

Carlo Dionisotti, professor of Italian at the University of London 1949–70 and a fellow of the British Academy from 1972, is commonly considered the greatest Italian literary historian of his age.[1] He had unrivalled expertise in fifteenth- and sixteenth-century Italian literature and a passionate interest in questions of Italian culture to which was added in his later years a particular insight into the nineteenth and twentieth centuries.

## 1. *Biography*

He was born on 9 June 1908 in Turin into a prosperous family.[2] His father, Eugenio (1866–1955), a graduate in law, was also Turinese. His paternal grandfather, Carlo (1824–1899), a magistrate and a historian, born in the nearby town of Vercelli, had studied and lived in Turin. Dionisotti, who was his namesake, was to mention with respect and affection the work of this grandfather.[3] His mother, Carla Cattaneo (1886–1973), was a Swiss national, born and bred in Italy. Dionisotti always felt a particular bond of affection with Italian-speaking Switzerland[4] and was to be a frequent visitor at Bigorio, outside Bellinzona, for the seminars regularly organized there by Swiss Italianists. In 1942 he married Maria Luisa (Marisa) Pinna Pintor, who belonged to a family among whose members we find a famous scholar and librarian, Fortunato Pintor (with whom Dionisotti became professionally linked when he worked for the *Dizionario biografico degli italiani* at the Istituto della Enciclopedia Italiana),[5] and Giaime Pintor, a much admired intellectual, who died in the fight against the Nazi-fascist regime in 1943.

Dionisotti's early education was peripatetic, owing to family moves during the First World War, but he received his secondary education in Turin at the Istituto Sociale directed by the Jesuits, to whom he was always grateful, notwithstanding his non-religious inclinations, for the good Latin grounding he received. He read arts (Lettere) at the University of Turin, where he graduated in 1929 with a thesis on Bembo's *Rime*, supervised by the professor of Italian literature, Vittorio Cian, a sixteenth-century specialist, and by Ferdinando Neri, professor of French literature. Dionisotti occasionally mentioned Cian in his writings with a certain detached respect and dutiful *pietas*, despite his dissent from the latter's fascist views and the difference in stature, since the pupil was superior to the teacher, both as a scholar and in intellectual calibre.[6] Dionisotti found Neri more congenial and warmly admired him.[7]

In Italy it was not uncommon at the time for schoolteaching to be the first stage in an academic career. In 1932, through a competitive examination, Dionisotti obtained a post to teach Latin and history at the Istituto Magistrale (Upper School for prospective teachers) at Vercelli and then in 1936 at the Istituto Magistrale Regina Margherita in Turin. He transferred to teach Italian and Latin in 1939 at the Liceo Cavour, also in Turin, and in 1941 at the Liceo Virgilio in Rome.

In 1937 Dionisotti had obtained the Libera Docenza (the Italian equivalent of the traditional German title of Privatdozent) and become the 'assistant' of Enrico Carrara, a specialist of Petrarch and of the Renaissance, at the Facoltà di Magistero. Subsequently, he was 'supplente' ('deputy professor') of the poet and bon vivant Francesco Pastonchi, whom the fascist regime had wished on the

University of Turin as its professor of Italian literature.[8] In Rome, as well as teaching at the Liceo Virgilio, in 1941–3 he worked for the Istituto della Enciclopedia Italiana; in 1943 he was posted ('comandato') to the Istituto di Studi Germanici, and in 1944, after the liberation of Rome, he became an 'assistant' to Natalino Sapegno, who held the chair of Italian literature in Rome.[9] In the same period he was an active journalist for the Resistance, with the Giustizia e Libertà movement and the Partito d'Azione, and associated with progressive publishing initiatives, including those of Einaudi, on which he collaborated with Cesare Pavese. He was a friend of Leone Ginzburg (one of the prime movers in the Einaudi publishing house), who died at Nazi-fascist hands in 1944.

In 1947 he took up the post of lecturer in Italian at the University of Oxford. The university archives hold an interesting file concerning his appointment.[10] There are three letters of reference. First, Roberto Weiss, professor of Italian at University College London, states that there is 'no doubt that Dionisotti occupies already a leading position among Italian students of the Renaissance,' and that 'his coming over to England would prove extremely beneficial to Italian scholarship in this country.' The second reference was written by James Wardrop, then assistant keeper at the Victoria and Albert Museum in London, who had known him for about ten years and stated that he had been impressed 'by the range and depth of Mr Dionisotti's scholarship, and by the humane and liberal direction he has given to his knowledge.' The fact that the war had ended shortly before explains in part some of the comments made in this letter of reference: 'Mr Dionisotti's entire dedication to culture and his opposition to anything which threatened its existence were not abated by his country's participation in the war; and the continued expression of his sympathies placed him – as I have reason to know – in situations of frequent difficulty and danger.' Interesting, also, are some observations about Dionisotti as a person: 'With equal confidence I can recommend Mr Dionisotti on the score of those personal qualities of courtesy, modesty and intellectual probity which would commend him to the society of his fellows in Oxford, should he be, as I hope, nominated to the Lectureship.' A third favourable, and more impersonal, reference was given by Ferdinando Neri, as dean of the Faculty of Letters in Turin in 1939–41.[11]

The file includes a correspondence with the Aliens' Department. In order to speed up the granting of a visa and a work permit, Douglas Veale, the university registrar, stressed the urgent need for a new lecturer, since there were twenty-eight students of Italian in autumn 1946, compared with seven the previous year, with only two teachers to instruct them (i.e., the professor, Alessandro Passerin d'Entrèves, and Miss Olga Bickley). Another interesting document is a detailed curriculum vitae of Dionisotti, including the mention of works at an advanced stage of preparation (some of which, however, apparently were never published, such as a volume on 'Pietro Bembo. Studi e documenti,' and a 'critical edition of Girolamo Fracastoro'). The c.v. is handwritten and unsigned, but the writing is clearly that of Arnaldo Momigliano, the famous ancient historian, who had been living in Oxford since 1938, when he had escaped from the anti-semitic laws in Italy. After war-time separation, he and Dionisotti, who had been students together, remained colleagues and close friends in Oxford and then in London, until Momigliano's death in 1987.[12]

In 1949 Professor d'Entrèves proposed that Dionisotti be given the title 'Reader' 'on the grounds of his high international reputation and of his extremely important services within the Italian Department.' In May, however, Dionisotti was elected, with effect from 1 October, to the chair of Italian at Bedford College, University of London, a position he held until 1970. After his retirement he had more opportunity to accept frequent invitations to lecture and participate in seminars and conferences in Italy, where he was highly admired and respected and received numerous honours and prizes.[13] He returned annually to the large family house at Romagnano Sesia (Novara), the village where he was eventually to be buried.

Dionisotti was a man of natural distinction. He was tall and slim. His expression and carriage were severe. He looked like someone who does not suffer fools gladly and he could be intimidating. He was respected, but also feared, among colleagues, who knew he could be ruthless in his criticism, particularly of people who were pompous and tried to conceal behind verbiage and nebulous theoretical jargon the poverty or shoddinesss of their scholarship. More generous towards the young, he could inspire devoted admiration. He was a dedicated teacher, but for some colleagues it was difficult to resist the impression that there was a lack of fit between what he could give (as one of the most formidable specialists on the Italian Renaissance) and what could be received (by the cohorts of pleasant undergraduates reading Italian at Bedford College).[14] He had few graduate students. One I should like to mention is Brian Richardson, whom he supervised for his master of philosophy thesis on Machiavelli and Livy and who went on to produce distinguished research on a characteristically Dionisottian topic, the importance of sixteenth-century editors in the establishment of the norm for the Italian literary language.[15]

Notwithstanding the severity of his appearance, Dionisotti could be excellent company, both humorous and entertaining. He was very generous and helpful, answering questions from colleagues and friends or commenting on what he happened to be working on if he thought it would be of interest.[16] He was also an extraordinary correspondent, punctually answering in handwritten letters and making precise and often original and valuable observations about offprints or books he had been sent, showing that he was an incredibly voracious and attentive reader right to the end of his life.[17]

Dionisotti wrote a vigorous Italian, sinewy and full of zest. He was a charismatic public speaker and an extremely vivacious and witty conversationalist. His speech, in both Italian and English, was unmistakably Piedmontese in rhythm, intonation, and phonological colouring. (Italian high culture at the University of London, in the decades when he was professor at Bedford and Momigliano at University College London, spoke with a Piedmontese accent.) He was alert to the difficulties connected with using a language not one's own, particularly in the tradition of Italian expatriates in Britain. He himself rarely published in English. In the nineteenth century, he observed, the British 'were generally smugly convinced that the linguistic barrier was as insuperable as that of the sea and of Her Majesty's fleet around the island, and that their language was safe from the impertinence of foreigners' (erano generalmente convinti e soddisfatti che insuperabile fosse la barriera linguistica, come quella del mare e della flotta di Sua Maestà intorno all'isola, e che insomma la loro lingua fosse al riparo dalla improntitudine degli stranieri).[18] They did acknowledge, however, that there were exceptions. One was Antonio Panizzi, the great editor of Boiardo and librarian of the British Museum, respected by Dionisotti[19] (partly because he was a paragon of seriousness and hard work – not the main qualities for which Italians were appreciated); but Panizzi's speech, both in English and in Italian, was 'incorrigible' (incorreggibile) in its Emilian pronunciation. Another exception was Antonio Gallenga, who 'wrote in a language not his own with diabolical ease and liveliness, unparalleled as far as I know in the history of Italians in England' (scriveva una lingua non sua con diabolica scioltezza e vivacità, senza riscontro, ch'io sappia, nella storia degli Italiani in Inghilterra). But he was not a man who earned Dionisotti's admiration, since 'Gallenga's linguistic ability included a good dose of Italian charlatanry' (l'abilità linguistica del Gallenga comportava una buona dose di italiana ciarlataneria). Also interesting is Dionisotti's attention to the way in which Italians spoke their own language:

> our experience teaches us that even today ... in Italy we cannot open our mouths without our pronunciation revealing our origin. It is probable that, as far as pronunciation is concerned, Manzoni's French was much better than his Italian. And there is an indirect and late (and therefore particularly striking) piece of evidence about Manzoni who in Florence 'called the proud Niccolini *Niculini* (with a broad Lombard *u* which seemed a scorpion with outspread nippers).'

> (l'esperienza nostra insegna che ancora oggi ... non possiamo in Italia aprire bocca senza che la pronunzia riveli la nostra origine. È probabile che, quanto a pronuncia, il francese di Manzoni fosse molto migliore del suo italiano. E una testimonianza è rimasta, indiretta e tarda, ma proprio per questo notevole, di lui che a Firenze 'chiamava Niculini (con tanto d'*u* lombardo che pareva uno scorpione a chele aperte) il fiero Niccolini.')

On other occasions we are reminded of Ascoli's difficulties with Italian usage or Paolo Marzolo's 'too marked dialectal Venetian pronunciation, acceptable in Milan, a parody in Naples' (troppo accentuata pronuncia dialettale veneta, sopportabile a Milano, caricaturale a Napoli).[20]

Although he lived in England from 1947 with his wife Marisa, and his three daughters grew up there,[21] Dionisotti was never assimilated into an active social life in that country and rarely saw his colleagues outside professional contexts. His personal friends were mostly Italians, some dating from school and university days in Turin. As well as his close friend Arnaldo Momigliano, one can recall writers such as Lalla Romano and Mario Soldati, the historians Federico Chabod and Franco Venturi, and scholars and intellectuals in many fields such as Giulio Einaudi, Alessandro Galante Garrone, Massimo Mila, Aldo Garosci, Giuseppe Billanovich, Augusto Campana, don Giuseppe De Luca, Umberto Bosco, Guido Martellotti, and others with whom he later established links, such as Marino Berengo, Domenico De Robertis, Alfredo Stussi, and the friends from the Ticino, such as Giovanni Pozzi.

He participated, with the distinction that could be expected from a man of his stature, in the activities required by his academic position in Britain, usually making them the occasion for the production of some memorable scholarly contribution, as when he gave the Taylorian Lecture on 'Europe in Sixteenth-Century Italian Literature' in 1971;[22] the Presidential Address of the Modern Humanities Research Association in 1972, on 'A Year's Work in the Seventies,' a brilliant discussion of scholarship in Italy in a European perspective against the background of political and social events of the 1870s;[23] and the British Academy lecture on 'Manzoni and the Catholic Revival' in 1973.[24] It was clear, however, that the natural cultural context for his scholarly production was Italy. It was in Italy that he was one of the founders and editors (from 1958), with Giuseppe Billanovich, Augusto Campana, and Paolo Sambin, of one of the main journals in his field, *Italia medioevale e umanistica*. In Italy, too, he was in close contact with friends such as Vittore Branca (who invited him to lecture at the Fondazione Cini in Venice), Gianfranco Contini, Maria Corti, Cesare Segre, and many others whose names would constitute a roll of honour for Italian studies. On his retirement Dionisotti received two Festschriften, both published in Italy.[25]

For many of the Italian academics who visited London to work at the British Museum Library, the trip was not complete without a conversation with Dionisotti, in one of the cafés near the

Museum. The opening of the new British Library was too late for him. In the last few years of his life he was more housebound, and friends from Italy went to see him at home at Golders' Green, where they found him, until the very end, as well informed, insatiably curious, and sharp-witted as ever. Yet the memory many will cherish of Dionisotti is of the reader at his desk, in the North Library and, in later years, when his interests had shifted from the sixteenth to the nineteenth century, in the Reading Room of the British Museum, sitting upright, reading with great concentration, and taking notes. Colleagues used to comment, only half-jocularly, that during over fifty years of nearly daily visits to the British Museum Library Dionisotti had read all the early printed books of its Italian collections. This was probably only a slight exaggeration. The image of Dionisotti that seems to me most appropriate is, in fact – more than that of the teacher, the editor, the author, or the public speaker – that of Dionisotti the reader.[26]

## 2. *Context*

If one tried to place Dionisotti's position within modern Italian culture, one could characterize him as an heir of the 'Scuola storica'[27] or historical school, which developed at the end of the nineteenth century, particularly at the University of Turin, through an emphasis on erudition and on a philological viewpoint, rather than on the interest, prevalent in Italy at the time, first in rhetorical formalism and then in the philosophical theories of Benedetto Croce's idealism. Dionisotti had great respect for Croce's erudition and the rich historical sense that made his works so worthwhile and instructive, but he disapproved of the facile adoption by his followers of idealistic attitudes that emphasized ready-made theoretical formulas at the expense of the concrete investigation of new historical facts, reliably established through competent use of paleography, printing history, metre, the conventions of literary genres, and all the other associated disciplines that Croceans disparagingly belittled as 'pseudosciences.'

For his part, Dionisotti was fully conversant with the relevant 'pseudosciences,' which are, in fact, the indispensable foundations and specialized tools of any serious literary study, and was scathing about the enthusiasm for vacuous 'problems' based on 'theoretical' assumptions, rather than for the more modest 'questions' one had to deal with in the course of empirical investigations.[28] He was very suspicious of trends and labels such as 'structuralism,' 'critical theory,' and 'deconstruction.' It is worth noting that it was at the very time, at the end of the 1960s, when French structuralism became a prevailing cultural movement, that the attitude that is summed up in the title of Dionisotti's book, *The Geography and History of Italian Literature* (*Geografia e storia della letturatura italiana*), acquired a remarkably deep resonance as a clarion call to study literary (and more generally cultural) facts, in the light of their specific, historical, chronological, and 'geographical' conditions. This felicitously titled volume of his collected essays brought Dionisotti to the attention of the general public in Italy and contributed to making him almost the personification of all the great Italians who, through their chosen exile, obtained insights they might not have reached at home.[29] It was this view from afar that allowed Dionisotti to formulate his thoughts with exceptional clarity, incisiveness, and persuasiveness.

The mention of 'geography' was, of course, particularly important within the Italian context, since it countered the ideologically and politically biased view of Italian national history that was dominant both in the Risorgimento (see, for instance, the powerful but misleading interpretation offered by Francesco De Sanctis's history of Italian literature) and in the nationalist assumptions adopted by fascism. Dionisotti's work stressed instead the fragmentation, the conflicts that characterized the history of Italian culture. Being a

Venetian or a Florentine, a Ferrarese or a Neapolitan, was a crucial, defining factor (differing, of course, according to historical circumstances), which could not and ought not to be seen as subordinate to the overarching feature of being Italian. If anything, it was the regional or even civic characterization that gave real meaning and substance to an otherwise too vague and general national label. It also had a contemporary resonance, since it stressed the importance and vitality of those regional traditions that had been publicly suppressed from the unification of the Italian state in 1861 to the fall of fascism in 1945, and were to remain only theoretically recognized for a long time after.

## 3. *Works*

Dionisotti's published output is impressive. It takes the form mainly of articles, which were often later collected into volumes. Further collections are now being prepared.[30] Also, there already exist some serviceable bibliographies of his publications.[31] In what follows I shall comment briefly on some of his books, in approximate chronological order, mentioning in particular their importance for the history of the Italian language, partly owing to my own interest in this aspect, but principally in view of the linguistic relevance of Dionisotti's 'geografia e storia' perspective and of the attention he devoted to Bembo, one of the protagonists of the 'questione della lingua' and a figure who was crucial to the subsequent direction taken by the Italian literary language.

In the 1930s he published important editions of Bembo's *Prose* and *Asolani e Rime*; these texts were later the basis of a volume of *Prose e rime*, with a new introduction, which enjoyed a notable success and several reprints.[32] It is still the most useful modern edition of Bembo's works. In 1945 he published, with an important introduction, Giovanni Guidiccioni's oration to the noblemen of Lucca, an interesting text about the insurrection of the 'straccioni' (literally 'the ragged') in the town in 1531.[33] In 1948 a formidable set of indices was printed, covering the first hundred volumes (for the years 1883–1932) of the *Giornale storico della letteratura italiana*, the main periodical representing the 'Scuola storica.'[34]

In 1949, together with Cecil Grayson (who, after having obtained a first in modern languages, had just started his teaching career at Oxford in 1948), he published a selection of *Early Italian Texts*, aimed at undergraduates and modest in appearance, but splendid for the good judgment and the solid scholarship on which both the choice of the texts and the philological introductions and commentary were based.[35] The book was deservedly well received, and not only in Britain. When I was a university student at Pisa in the mid-1950s, this was one of the textbooks we used for our examination on the history of the Italian language, and even now, over fifty years after its publication, it ranks among the most useful collections one can recommend to students of early Italian. In 1950 Dionisotti published, with a rich introduction, an edition of Maria Savorgnan's love letters to Bembo.[36]

An interesting contribution is the second edition (1952) of the elegant *Oxford Book of Italian Verse* originally published in 1910 by St John Lucas.[37] In the Oxford syllabus of the early 1950s Italian literature still ended in 1860. Dionisotti increased the total number of poems from 345 to 376, adding some names in the body of the anthology and at the end and eliminating certain others.[38] The criteria mentioned by Dionisotti in the preface are worth quoting: 'It might be remembered that this is a book of Italian verse, that is to say of poems which were written in what is considered to be the Italian language. Italian poets who wrote either in Latin or in one or other of the Italian dialects had to be set aside' (vi). On the one hand, this decision may appear simply as common sense: poems written in Latin or in dialect are not suitable for foreign readers of a 'Book of Italian Verse.' On the other, we should avoid the temptation to read into this statement a restrictive definition of what can be said to belong to Italian literature. On the contrary, we must remember that merely three years before, in delivering his trailblazing inaugural lecture at Bedford College, Dionisotti had stressed the multilingual nature of Italian literature, and it is this awareness that allows him to avoid the blurring of linguistic distinctions and enables him instead to differentiate clearly between poems written in 'what is considered to be the Italian language,' and those written in other languages, by authors who were nevertheless still 'Italian poets.'

Dionisotti's name is linked, above all, with his book on the geography and history of Italian literature.[39] This volume includes nine memorable essays published separately between 1946 and 1966. They are preceded by a preface in which Dionisotti dedicates the volume to 'the first of his friends,' Aldo Garosci, together with the companions of their youth in Turin. When they were university students, the city was of course no longer that of Gobetti and Gramsci, the great figures, respectively, of the liberal and of the communist opposition to fascism. Fascist dictatorship had prevailed in Turin as in the rest of Italy, and independently minded intellectuals could only look abroad, or to the past, if they wanted to nourish the hope of a new Italy capable of reviving the Medieval and Renaissance traditions which had made such a crucial contribution to the common heritage of European civilization. Dionisotti presents his work as witness of 'an enquiry carried out with respect for the truth but also with political passion' (una inchiesta condotta con scrupolo di verità, ma con passione politica). Among the most powerful of these essays is the eponymous one ([1951] 1967, 23–45) I mentioned above (see n. 29) in which he questions the 'unitary line' (linea unitaria) generally followed in tracing the history of Italian literature and develops in particular the aspect he calls 'linguistic polyvalence' (polivalenza linguistica), resulting from the coexistence of Latin, Provençal, French and Tuscan traditions, as well as the 'dialect' aspects. The third essay, 'Chierici e laici' ([1960] 1967, 47–73)[40] presents a strikingly enlightening outline, such as had never been attempted before, of the history of Italian literature from the viewpoint of the distinction between clergy and laity: clerics were among the main exponents of Italian letters until the end of the eighteenth century, but the situation changed with the establishment of lay education after the French revolution.[41] Previously, secular initiative had been crucial to the emergence of vernacular literature, among the Sicilians in the thirteenth century with Dante, and between the fourteenth and fifteenth centuries with the crisis of the Church in the age of the Schism and the great humanists working for the State. Otherwise, it was the Church, through religious orders, ecclesiastical benefits, placements as bishops and cardinals, that offered men of letters security, a degree of independence, and general living conditions preferable to those offered by other employments. The image of Italian literature conveyed by traditional nineteenth- and twentieth-century historiography ignores almost completely or gives an insufficient account of the centrality of the Church for Italian men of letters.

In the fourth essay, 'Per una storia della lingua italiana' ([1962] 1967, 75–102),[42] Dionisotti offers a synthetic account, based on a review of the book by Bruno Migliorini, which is still the most informative, solid, and reliable presentation of the history of the Italian language, chronologically structured, and with individual chapters devoted to successive centuries. Dionisotti takes the opportunity to illustrate the importance of language for his 'geografia e storia' view of the Italian tradition. On the one hand, during the fourteenth century there was the victory, sudden and definitive, of Tuscan over the other regional vernaculars and therefore the birth of the Italian national literary language. On the other, the dialects live on, as spoken languages, until the twentieth century and beyond. This dichotomy contributes to explaining the static, formal perfection of literary Italian, the scarcity of what is known about the history of spoken Italian (in contrast to the dialects), and the interesting fact that, for instance, humanistic literature in Latin, in the late quattrocento, is more 'popular' and 'realistic' than its vernacular counterpart.

Similar points are made, with great vigour and extraordinary erudition, in the chapters of the slim volume *Gli umanisti e il volgare* (see n. 6). Here Dionisotti stresses the importance of the newly developed interest in Greek, with its variety of literary dialects (in contrast to the unitary character of Latin) for the discussions on the 'questione della lingua,' even though Bembo's solution finally imposed a unitary standard comparable to the Ciceronian one that prevailed for Latin.

Other important collections are the volumes that brought together the essays on Machiavelli;[43] those on Foscolo, Pietro Giordani, Leopardi, Manzoni, Nievo (as well as other striking articles, 'Piemontesi e spiemontizzati,' which opens the book, and 'Ricordo di Quintino Sella,' which closes it);[44] those on Aldo Manuzio;[45] those on Leonardo, Giorgione, Titian, Vasari, Battista Fiera,[46] Francesco Colonna, Niccolò Liburnio, Pirro Ligorio, G.B. Marino, and other authors relevant to the relation between artists and men of letters.[47] An impressive selection, prepared by Dionisotti and published after his death, is *Ricordi della scuola italiana*. It includes thirty-six articles devoted to authors and episodes in Italian culture from the eighteenth to the twentieth century. Among the most rewarding are those on Antonio Panizzi ([1979, 1980] 1998, 179–276), on Graziadio Ascoli and the discussions on the Italian language after unification ([1991, 1993] 1998, 277–314), and on Alessandro D'Ancona's correspondence ([1976] 1998, 321–68).[48]

## 4. Conclusion

I should like to observe, finally, that one impression Dionisotti could make (and did make on some colleagues) was of a man of the nineteenth century – almost a figure of the Italian Risorgimento, one of those serious, upright, irreproachable Piedmontese 'tutti d'un pezzo' who contributed so much to the formation of an Italian national ideal (if not with equal success to the effective reality of the new state), whom Dionisotti admired and whose memory he helped to keep alive. Yet this view does not do justice to the sense of emotional, passionate involvement with the present that one senses in Dionisotti's work. His distaste for fashionable cultural trends was based not on lack of interest for things modern but rather on an uncompromising hostility towards attitudes he considered frivolous or wanting in commitment to truth and objectivity as irreducible values in historical research.

This conviction had its political counterpart in his espousal of the line of Giustizia e Libertà, the anti-fascist left-liberal movement, distant from both Catholic and communist positions. Characteristic of Dionisotti's ideas on the responsibility of intellectuals were the comments he made (and did not hesitate to repeat and elaborate on in later years) on the killing of Giovanni Gentile, the famous philosopher and cultural organizer, president of the Enciclopedia Italiana Institute, who completely identified himself with the fascist regime. He was killed (murdered or executed, depending on the viewpoint), almost certainly by communist partisans, in Florence, on 15 April 1944. His death caused an enormous sensation among Italian intellectuals, many of whom (including those who were politically not on his side) appreciated his human qualities and personal honesty. Dionisotti wrote in the *Nuovi Quaderni di Giustizia e Libertà*, an article in which he 'explained' the killing in the pitiless light of the savage civil war being fought in Italy at the time – a war in which it was impossible, and in any case would have been morally unacceptable, not to take sides; a war the ferocity of which was not unfamiliar to historians of medieval and Renaissance Italy.[49] The passionate anti-fascist who intervened on that burning political and ideological question was of a piece with the dispassionate scholar who spent most of his life in the British Library investigating and bringing back to life figures and texts from Italy's past.[50]

NOTES

1  This chapter was published originally in the *Proceedings of the British Academy*, vol. 11 (2000). I am grateful to Anna Carlotta Dionisotti and Luigi Meneghello for help and advice.

2  The surname 'Casalone,' which followed his own in his first publications, is that of a family friend who wished his own name to survive, in association with that of Dionisotti.

3  Carlo Dionisotti, *Appunti sui moderni: Foscolo, Leopardi, Manzoni e altri* (Bologna: il Mulino, 1988), 388–91. He also wrote a preface to to the reprint of a book of his grandfather Carlo (originally Turin: Tip. Favale, 1871), *La Vallesesia ed il Comune di Romagnano-Sesia* (Novara: Paltrinieri, 1972), 3–12.

4  See the dedication of *Appunti sui moderni*, 8: 'I dedicate this book, belated token of gratitude and affection, to Giulia Gianella of Bellinzona, and with her to all my other friends of Italian Switzerland who have helped me back and forth over the frontier. And not only the one that divides the Confederation from the Republic' (Dedico il libro, tardo pegno di riconoscenza e di affetto, a Giulia Gianella di Bellinzona e con lei agli amici tutti della Svizzera Italiana, che mi hanno aiutato a passare, avanti e indietro, la frontiera. Non soltanto quella che divide la Confederazione dalla Repubblica). See also Carlo Dionisotti, 'Una Svizzera che vive,' in Giuseppe Billanovich, Carlo Dionisotti, Dante Isella, and Giovanni Pozzi, *Maestri italiani a Friburgo (da Arcari a Contini e dopo)* (Locarno: Armando Dadò, 1998), 9–12. The lecture given by Dionisotti in Bâle to students and colleagues in 1994, before the conferment of a doctorate *honoris causa*, can be read in Carlo Dionisotti, 'Un'Italia fra Svizzera e Inghilterra (con una nota di Maria Antonietta Terzoli),' *Giornale storico della letteratura italiana* 178 (2001), 194–204. It was also published, together with other

useful documents, in Dionisotti, *Un'Italia tra Svizzera e Inghilterra*. A cura di Maria Antonietta Terzoli. Con un'intervista di Fausto Gimondi (Bellinzona: Casagrande, 2002).

5  See the memoir in Carlo Dionisotti, *Ricordi della scuola italiana* (Rome: Edizioni di Storia e Letteratura, 1998), 461–7.

6  On Cian see the entry by Piero Treves, in *Dizionario biografico degli italiani*, vol. 25 (Rome: Istituto della Enciclopedia Italiana, 1981), 155–60. For Dionisotti's attitude, see his *Gli umanisti e il volgare fra Quattro e Cinquecento* (Florence: Le Monnier, 1968), 41–3; Università degli Studi della Calabria, *Laurea Honoris Causa a Carlo Dionisotti 15 dicembre 1994* (Soveria Mannelli: Rubbettino, 1996), 50–1.

7  On Ferdinando Neri see Dionisotti, *Ricordi*, 328–32; Università degli Studi della Calabria, *Laurea*, 55–7.

8  On Pastonchi see Carlo Dionisotti, *Lettere londinesi (1968–1995)*, ed. Giuseppe Anceschi (Florence: Olschki, 2000), 16–17; and Dionisotti, *Ricordi*, 475.

9  See Carlo Dionisotti, *Natalino Sapegno dalla Torino di Gobetti alla cattedra romana*, con un'appendice di scritti di Natalino Sapegno. Lezione Sapegno 1994 (Turin: Bollati Boringhieri, 1994); and *Ricordi*, 477–88.

10  I have consulted the relevant file (Oxford University Archives, FA9/1/91) at the Bodleian Library. I am grateful to my friend Diego Zancani of Balliol College who transcribed the relevant documents for me. For more information see the letters published by Vincenzo Fera as an appendix to his article, 'Tra piemontesi ad Oxford: La lectureship di Dionisotti,' in *Carlo Dionisotti: Geografia e storia di uno studioso*, ed. Edoardo Fumagalli (Rome: Edizioni di storia e letteratura, 2001), 69–118. The papers presented at the Freiburg conference on Dionisotti, 15 April 1999, are published in the Fumagalli volume.

11  Dionisotti mentions in *Ricordi*, 495, that he had been 'introduced and recommended' (presentato e raccomandato) also by Benedetto Croce, for his teaching post at Oxford. The letter is not in the Oxford file. Croce had, in fact, written to Passerin d'Entrèves who was able to mention this in the discussions concerning the appointment. See Fera, 'Tra piemontesi ad Oxford.'

12  See Carlo Dionisotti, *Ricordo di Arnaldo Momigliano* (Bologna: Il Mulino, 1989); also *Ricordi*, 587–604.

13  He was a member of the Accademia delle Scienze di Torino, of the Accademia Nazionale dei Lincei, of the Arcadia of Rome. He was awarded the Premio Viareggio in 1989, and he received an honorary doctorate from the University of Calabria in 1994 (see above, n. 4).

14 For Dionisotti as a teacher, see Nelia Saxby, Appendix in Brian Richardson, 'Carlo Dionisotti,' *Italian Studies* 54 (1999), 13–17, 16–17.

15 See Brian Richardson's volume *Print Culture in Renaissance Italy: The Editor and the Vernacular Text, 1470–1600* (Cambridge: Cambridge University Press, 1994), in which Dionisotti is by far the most frequently cited among modern scholars. See also the above cited obituary by Richardson, 'Carlo Dionisotti.'

16 I remember, for instance, one case in which he came to my seat at the North Library to show me, with a smile, a passage from *Idea della storia dell'Italia letterata* (Naples: Felice Mosca, 1723), written by a minor Italian eighteenth-century erudite, Giacinto Gimma, about the use of 'a metaphorical signifier over a true signified' (un significante metaforico sopra un significato vero). The use of 'significante' and 'significato' in 1723 was, in fact, remarkable; the smile that accompanied the quote was a teasing suggestion that I might interpret the passage in the perspective of Saussurean ideas, while he was (correctly) placing it within its own historical context (*Ricordi*, 17–19).

17 For a striking example see chapter five in this volume.

18 *Ricordi*, 184.

19 Although he observed that some of his human traits were less than admirable; see *Ricordi*, 197–8, 208.

20 *Ricordi*, 210, 188, 309, 281, 283, 287.

21 The eldest, Anna Carlotta, teaches classics at King's College London; the second, Paola, is a well-known actress; the third, Eugenia, is a librarian.

22 Carlo Dionisotti, *Europe in Sixteenth-Century Italian Literature: The Taylorian Lecture Delivered 11 February 1971* (Oxford: Clarendon Press, 1971).

23 Carlo Dionisotti, 'A Year's Work in the Seventies: The Presidential Address of the Modern Humanities Research Association Delivered at University College London on 7 January 1972,' *Modern Language Review* 67 (1972), xix–xxviii.

24 Carlo Dionisotti, 'Manzoni and the Catholic Revival,' *Proceedings of the British Academy* 59 (1973), 341–53. For these lectures see Carlo Dionisotti, *Lezioni inglesi* (Turin: Aragno, 2001).

25 *Studi di filologia e di letteratura italiana offerti a Carlo Dionisotti*, ed. Istituto di Letteratura e Filologia Italiana of the University of Pavia (Milan-Naples: Ricciardi, 1973); *Tra latino e volgare: Per Carlo Dionisotti*, ed. Gabriella Bernardoni Trezzini et al., 2 vols (Padua: Antenore, 1974). The editors of the latter book were members of the Bigorio group.

26 It is appropriate to remember here the words from Horace that Dionisotti was fond of quoting, 'cui lecta potenter erit res'; see *Geografia e storia della letteratura italiana* (Turin: Einaudi, 1967), 103. This has been sometimes play-

fully interpreted as an invitation to 'read powerfully,' rather than in the original sense it has in Horace of selecting (legere) the subject (res) according to one's power (potenter). See the observations in Giuseppe Fumagalli, *Chi l'ha detto?* 10th ed. (Milan: Hoepli, 1968), 499–500 (N. 1663).

27 See Dionisotti's article, 'Scuola storica,' in Vittore Branca, ed., *Dizionario critico della letteratura italiana*, vol. 4 (Turin: UTET, 1986), 139–48; and *Ricordi*, 393.

28 See the comments by Dionisotti in *Geografia e storia*, 89–90: 'Migliorini's *Storia* is, as one might expect, an honest, sound, useful and, thank God, unproblematic book. ... We had to proceed for most of our lives with difficulty, short of breath, in an atmosphere thick with problems: "He removed from before his face that thick air frequently moving his left hand before him"' (La *Storia* di Migliorini è, quale poteva attendersi, un libro onesto, sano, utile, e, grazie a Dio, non problematico ... Abbiamo dovuto avanzare tutto il tempo di nostra vita a stento, col fiato mozzo, in un'aria densa di problemi: 'Dal volto rimovea quell'aere grasso, menando la sinistra innanzi spesso'). The quote from Dante's *Inferno*, canto 9, 82–3, refers to the Messenger from Heaven removing from before his face the dense air of Hell. As for these 'problems,' they were expected to be resolved by the latest interpreter 'equipped not with the vulgar tools of linguistic and historical enquiry, but with his presumptuous little soul and with the philosopher's stone that he happened to have in his hand, consisting of a perfect aesthetic doctrine and critical methodology' (munito, non dei volgari strumenti dell'indagine linguistica e storica, ma della sua *animula* presuntuosa e della pietra filosofale, che fortunosamente si trovava ad avere in mano, di una perfetta dottrina estetica e metodologia critica).

29 'Geografia e storia della letteratura italiana,' *Italian Studies* 6 (1951), 70–93; also published in *Geografia e storia*, 23–45. This essay was based on the Inaugural Lecture for the Chair of Italian at Bedford College, given on 22 November 1949.

30 *Scritti sul Bembo*, ed. Claudio Vela, and *Scritti civili*, ed. Ersilia Alessandrone Perona and Giorgio Panizza (Turin: Einaudi, forthcoming).

31 Giulia Gianella, 'Bibliografia degli scritti di Carlo Dionisotti,' in *Tra latino e volgare*, vol. 1, xvii–xxxii; Mirella Ferrari, 'In memoria di Carlo Dionisotti (1908–1998): Bibliografia,' *Aevum* 72 (1998), 817–46. A revised and updated version of the latter appeared in Fumagalli, *Carlo Dionisotti*, 151–95.

32 Pietro Bembo, *Prose della volgar lingua*, introduction and notes by Carlo Dionisotti Casalone (Turin: UTET, 1931); *Gli Asolani e le Rime*, introduction

and notes by Carlo Dionisotti Casalone (Turin: UTET, 1932); *Prose e rime*, ed. Carlo Dionisotti (Turin: UTET, 1960; 2nd ed. 1966).

33 Giovanni Guidiccioni, *Orazione ai nobili di Lucca*, ed. Carlo Dionisotti (Rome: Edizioni di Storia e Letteratura, 1945). New edition (Milan: Adelphi, 1994).

34 *Indici del 'Giornale storico della letteratura italiana.' Volumi 1–100 e supplementi 1883–1932*, ed. Carlo Dionisotti (Turin: Chiantore, 1948).

35 *Early Italian Texts*, ed. with notes by Carlo Dionisotti and Cecil Grayson (Oxford: Blackwell, 1949; new edition, 1965).

36 Maria Savorgnan – Pietro Bembo, *Carteggio d'amore (1500–1501)*, ed. Carlo Dionisotti (Florence: Le Monnier, 1950).

37 *The Oxford Book of Italian Verse, XIIIth Century – XIXth Century*, chosen by St John Lucas, 2nd ed. rev. with twentieth-century supplement by Carlo Dionisotti (Oxford: Clarendon Press, 1952).

38 He added to the body of the text: L.B. Alberti, Gianni Alfani, T. Campanella, Cariteo (B. Gareth), F. Della Valle, G. Fantoni, G.A. Petrucci, A. Pucci, O. Rinuccini, L. Savioli Fontana, G.B. Strozzi, L. Tornabuoni de' Medici, and G. Zanella; at the end he included G. Pascoli, V. Aganoor, G. D'Annunzio, G. Gozzano, S. Corazzini, and C. Michelstaedter; those deleted were Ciullo/ Cielo d'Alcamo, Federico II, Re Enzo, Anselmo da Ferrara, A. Caro, B. Rota, A. Tassoni, F.A. Ghedini, P. Manara, A. Mazza, L. Carrer, and F. dall'Ongaro.

39 *Geografia e storia*. The volume was later published in the Piccola Biblioteca Einaudi 163 (Turin: Einaudi, 1971; 11th reprint 1999).

40 Originally published as 'Chierici e laici nella letteratura italiana del primo Cinquecento,' in *Problemi di vita religiosa in Italia nel Cinquecento: Atti del Convegno di Storia della Chiesa in Italia, Bologna, 2–6 sett. 1958* (Padua: Antenore, 1960), 167–85. It was later published in a new edition: *Chierici e laici*, con una lettera di Delio Cantimori, introduction by Roberto Cicala (Novara: Interlinea edizioni, 1995).

41 Dionisotti, in an article published in 1991 (*Ricordi*, 515), stresses the link between his historical research and his present experience. He explains how he was moved to investigate the question of 'clerics and laymen' (chierici e laici) by the prevalence in post-war Italy of a political party backed by the Catholic Church, 'a prevalence which my forebears and my party in Piedmont would have never thought possible,' (una prevalenza che i miei primi e la mia parte in Piemonte mai avrebbero creduto possibile); but even earlier, during the war, he was led to question his previous assumptions, when, in the general collapse of the Italian state, the Church structures had proved themselves stronger and

more deeply rooted than the civic ones. This had made him look afresh at the relation between 'chierici' and 'laici' throughout the history of Italian culture.

42  The review originally appeared in *Romance Philology* 16 (1962), 41–58.

43  Carlo Dionisotti, *Machiavellerie* (Turin: Einaudi, 1980), including important studies not previously published.

44  Dionisotti, *Appunti sui moderni*.

45  Carlo Dionisotti, *Aldo Manuzio, umanista e editore* (Milan: Edizioni il Polifilo, 1995).

46  Battista Fiera had been studied by James Wardrop. The warm appreciation manifested in the reference for Dionisotti (mentioned above) was reciprocated, as can be seen from the moving and elegant expressions in Carlo Dionisotti, *Appunti su arti e lettere* (Milan: Jaca Book, 1995), 57–8.

47  Dionisotti, *Appunti su arti e lettere*.

48  Dionisotti, *Ricordi*; essays originally published in 1976, 1979, 1980, 1991, and 1993.

49  Carlo Dionisotti, 'Giovanni Gentile,' *Nuovi Quaderni di Giustizia e Libertà* (May–June 1944), 86–95. Reprinted in *L'Indice dei Libri del mese* 2:9 (1985), 23–6; also, 'La morte amara di Gentile,' *Resistenza: Giustizia e Libertà*, 18:4 (1964), 1.

50  Among the obituaries and profiles, I should like to mention Verina R. Jones, 'Ricordo di Carlo Dionisotti,' *Annali Manzoniani*, new ser. 3 (1999), 427–31; Anna Laura Lepschy and Giulio Lepschy, 'Carlo Dionisotti (A Personal Appreciation),' *The Italianist* 18 (1998), 5–9; Giulio Lepschy, 'Ricordo di Carlo Dionisotti,' *Rinascimento* 99 (1999), 119–25; Richardson, 'Carlo Dionisotti'; Alfredo Stussi, 'Ricordo di Carlo Dionisotti,' *Intersezioni* 18 (1998), 379–88; Claudia Villa, 'Ricordo di Carlo Dionisotti,' *Belfagor* 54 (1999), 61–9. See also Villa, 'Carlo Dionisotti' (Ritratti critici di contemporanei), *Belfagor* 43 (1988), 49–65.

# Index